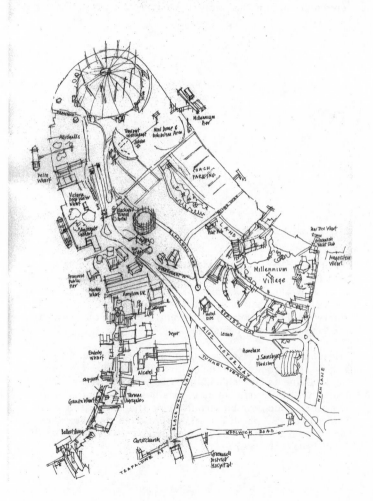

Production of this book has been supported by Docklands Forum. The Forum has worked in east London since the early 1970s, when industrial decline meant that new opportunities must be grasped – but that the process of this change needed to be monitored and communities supported in a process which was not always easy.

Cover illustrations and end papers by Peter Kent.

Front: Peter Kent's overview of the Greenwich Peninsula tries to visualise how industry might have looked. The South Metropolitan Gas Works occupied most of the eastern shore line while to the west a multitude of industries thrived alongside the working wharves. The entrance to Blackwall Tunnel and the giant gas holders are easily recognisable.

Back: Peter Kent's visualisation of the Greenwich Peninsula as it might look at the turn of the century. Industry has been replaced by the Dome and the Millennium Village on the eastern shore line, while the diversity of industry still survives on the western riverside - much can be seen from the Thames Path. The entrance to the Blackwall Tunnel and its adjoined gasholder can be clearly seen and is useful for comparison with the image on the final pages of the book.

GREENWICH MARSH THE 300 YEARS BEFORE THE DOME

Mary Mills

First published in Great Britain in 1999 by
M.Wright, 24 Humber Road, London, SE3 7LT.
© 1999 Mary Mills

ISBN: 0 9535245 0 7

Printed and bound in Great Britain by Biddles Ltd., Guildford
and Kings Lynn

CONTENTS

ILLUSTRATIONS

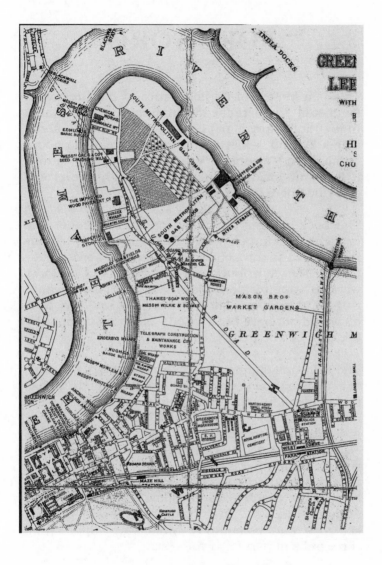

FOREWORD

This is a history of the industries of the Greenwich
Peninsula - where the Millennium Dome will stand.
Industrial history is not boring – it is, after all, about
ingenuity and achievement - sometimes it is about
criminal and/or eccentric behaviour and, of course,
it is about making money. Frequently the events
described here have touched everyone's lives.

This book is about the innovators and inventors who
brought their processes to East Greenwich usually
in order to manufacture things and to prosper by
them. The contribution of generations of ordinary
workers and residents is very important because
without them the money (which they saw very little
of) would not have been made – but it needs another
book, or books, to do them justice.

The following chapters make up a very brief resume
of activity on the Peninsula. A great deal of detail has
had to be omitted in order to make the finished work
of a reasonable size. Fuller accounts of many
individual subjects have appeared as journal articles
elsewhere - and are listed in the bibliography. Some
very important items have been left out for the same
reason - in particular the Blackwall Tunnel, the
trams and the A102M road as well as two local
authority depots. There is no mention of housing
schemes and community buildings - apart from
three pubs of particular interest.

In order to improve accessibility a policy has been
adopted of only footnoting some direct quotations. If
any reader would like a fully annotated academic-
style text of any section or any references please
contact the author and it can be supplied at cost
price per sheet.   It is also to be regretted that,
through lack of finance, so few pictures from the
hundreds available can be used.

Greenwich marsh has been owned mainly by charities since the seventeenth century.   It is valuable
land and has been exploited for commerce.   These
charities saw the investment potential of sites near
the capital city and with excellent access to the River
and trade routes.

From around 1800 riverside areas of the marsh were
developed and industry moved in at a rapidly increasing pace until around the time of the Overend
Gurney banking crash of 1866. From the 1870s the
pace began to slacken and in the twentieth century
there was a long slide into service industries which
themselves collapsed as the upriver docks closed in
the 1960s and 1970s. In the 1990s we have the
Millennium Dome.

The Dome may well mark a change in the fortunes of
the area - while, at the same time, it is part of a
continuum of change and innovation - but you need
to read this book to find that out.

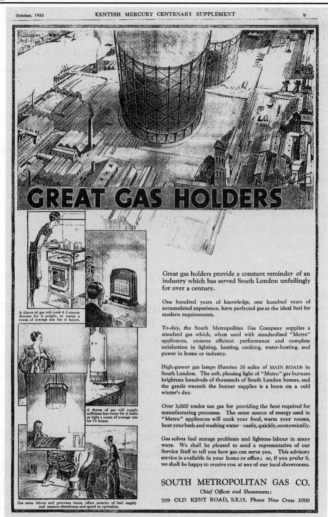

GREAT GAS HOLDERS

A therm of gas will cook 6 2-course dinners for 6 people, or warm a room of average size for 6 hours.

A therm of gas will supply sufficient hot water for 6 baths or light a room of average size for 72 hours.

Gas saves labour and prevents waste, offers security of fuel supply and ensures cleanliness and speed in operation.

Great gas holders provide a constant reminder of an industry which has served South London unfailingly for over a century.

One hundred years of knowledge, one hundred years of accumulated experience, have perfected gas as the ideal fuel for modern requirements.

To-day, the South Metropolitan Gas Company supplies a standard gas which, when used with standardised "Metro" appliances, ensures efficient performance and complete satisfaction in lighting, heating, cooking, water-heating, and power in home or industry.

High-power gas lamps illumine 26 miles of MAIN ROADS in South London. The soft, pleasing light of "Metro" gas burners brightens hundreds of thousands of South London homes, and the gentle warmth the burner supplies is a boon on a cold winter's day.

Over 3,000 trades use gas for providing the heat required for manufacturing processes. The same source of energy used in "Metro" appliances will cook your food, warm your rooms, heat your bath and washing water—easily, quickly, economically.

Gas solves fuel storage problems and lightens labour in many ways. We shall be pleased to send a representative of our Service Staff to tell you how gas can serve you. This advisory service is available in your home or office; or, if you prefer it, we shall be happy to receive you at any of our local showrooms.

SOUTH METROPOLITAN GAS CO.

Chief Offices and Showrooms:

709 OLD KENT ROAD, S.E.15. Phone New Cross 2000

An advertisement for the South Metropolitan Gas Co. printed by Kentish Mercury for their centenary in 1933. The gas holders are pictured with all the verve and confidence typical of South Met.

1. GREENWICH MARSH

The Greenwich Peninsula used to be called Greenwich Level - because a marsh is what it was - and
what it still is, and a 'level' because it is flat. Before
1800 it was the most upriver point of the bleak and
beautiful marshes on the south side of the Thames
estuary - a place of *wet land and dry water*.[1]

The area that the marsh covers is easily defined.
The loops of the Thames as it winds between London
and its estuary, are very clear on any relevant map.
One such loop defines a finger of land projecting
from the southern shore east of Greenwich so that
the River forms a long main boundary to north, east
and west. A southern boundary is neatly defined by
the main road between Greenwich and Woolwich. An
eastern land boundary is formed by Horn Lane,
parallel to a sixteenth century flood barrier called
Lambarde's Wall - which is also the Greenwich
parish boundary.

Until the late nineteenth century Greenwich was
part of the county of Kent - so its inclusion in

London is, in terms of its long history comparatively recent. Proximity to the capital helped determine how the land was used. The most northerly point of the Peninsula was once known as Lea Ness – the 'nose' of land facing Bow Creek, which is the winding estuary of the river Lea flowing south and emerging on the north bank of the Thames. More recently it has been known as 'Blackwall Point'.... Black Wall being the sea 'wall' on the eastern side of the Isle of Dogs – Mill Wall is on the west side where there were a number of windmills.

Through the mediaeval period Greenwich marsh was within 'The Manor of Old Court'. By the sixteenth century most of which was owned by the Crown and within the next hundred years, with some small exceptions, it had passed into the hands of charities, which leased land out to whoever wanted to use it. They are the bodies who have shaped the present.

THE MARSH SINCE 1315

The marsh has been drained and managed for so long that it is difficult to imagine what it looked like a thousand years ago - or what it would be now without constant care and maintenance. In 1315 a Commission was set up to look after the river wall and ditches. From the early seventeenth century management of the area was undertaken by the 'Court of Sewers' and the minutes of their meetings, dating from 1625, are held in a local library. This body was made up of representatives of landowners and their tenants. Every year they would walk round the area and note what work was needed - ditches to be cleaned, brambles to be cut back and repairs to be made. Work was paid for through the Wallscot tax and non-payers were fined. A bailiff was employed to get the work done. The Court continued with its work for over 200 years until its duties were taken over by Greenwich Board of Works and the London County Council.

On seventeenth century maps a lane is shown running through the marsh. It left the Woolwich Road at the Ship and Billet pub (today The Frog and Radiator). Marsh Lane went north from the Woolwich Road and then divided into two - one arm went east towards the River and the other went straight ahead. These lanes were still there until the coming of the Dome, and anyone who has walked the area knows it as Blackwall Lane, and the easterly arm which was also known as Marsh Lane, and, more recently, Riverway.   On the east, running straight between Woolwich Road and the river is Horn Lane.

The marsh was made up fields - the boundaries of many of them still make up the areas of the factories, which were later built on them. Their names have now entirely disappeared - among them were The Pitts, Balsopps, Goose Marsh and Cat's Brains. We can only speculate on why they were given.

By 1625 the most important work had been done towards establishing a drainage system, in order to allow the land to be used for farming and similar pursuits. Bendish Sluice emerged by Enderby's

Wharf; Arnold's Sluice entered the Thames to the north east of Blackwall Point; King's Sluice was near Horn Lane and there was another to the south west of Blackwall Point. These sluices were a major civil engineering project carried out by experts whose names may never be discovered. It is thought that they were Dutch. Without them the Peninsula would not exist in the form it does today.

THE SEA WALL

The other major work done before records began was the building of the seawall. It was called the 'sea wall' not the 'river wall' because of the power of the tidal river and the strength needed to hold it back. So important was - and is - care and maintenance of the wall that local taxes were called the 'wallscot'.

Before 1625, the River broke its banks and the result was 'Horseshoe Breach', which was never repaired and is still there today. There was a constant sense of urgency in case a storm should lead to another such disaster. A few dangerously high tides would quickly lead to calls for something to be done.

A number of well-known engineers worked on the wall. In the late 1820s a serious problem arose on the west bank. The top civil engineers of the day were asked for their opinions. Thomas Telford thought the problems were caused by the large number of ships using the recently opened West India Docks. The Court of Sewers had great difficulty in raising the money to pay him even though an arrangement had been made with the wealthy charity, Morden College, to buy some of the land affected. They later refused to pay John Rennie, Jnr. also brought in as a consultant, and his arrogant complaint *'Nothing annoys me so much as disputes about payment'*[2] did nothing to improve relationships. Telford eventually undertook the job and his work lies somewhere on the west bank at the northern end of the Peninsula.

There were other problems with the sea wall and the riverbank. For instance throughout the nineteenth century the Court of Sewers accused the lightermen who worked for Trinity House and the Corporation of the City of London of removing stone from the sea wall to use as ballast – something always denied by the authorities concerned. Conversely in 1843 it was proposed to dump mud, excavated from the West India Dock on the wall itself. As late as 1890 a firm was operating a 'mud shute' there.

EARLY BUILDINGS

Before 1800 little was built on the marsh beyond a few sheds and barns. No one lived there and for many years there were gates with a gatekeeper to stop casual visitors. A watch house, or perhaps a building connected with river defences, was built in the middle of the Marsh. It was in what could be described as the 'bottom centre' of the Marsh, an area later known as 'House Marsh'. It is possible, but unlikely, that this might have something to do with Tudor defences. At one time there a watchman was employed – and in any case a depot of some sort would have been needed by the marsh bailiff and his staff – somewhere to keep their tools, and provide some shelter for meal breaks and during bad weather.

The one major building was the Gunpowder Depot – of which more later. The military guard on it probably deterred much trespass – although the Court of Sewers complained bitterly about the behaviour of soldiers posted there. Even after 1800 few people lived in the area - apart from the little community in the east, around The Pilot pub, which grew up after 1802. In the south part of the marsh in the area adjacent to the Woolwich Road, housing of a good standard was provided under the supervision of Morden College from the 1840s and this area is still flourishing. In the late nineteenth century a number of factories provided homes for their workers and some speculative housing was built. Most of the people who lived there probably had little choice but to put up with damp conditions in what was still a down-market area.

Gradually amenities were built - a church, mission halls, shops, more pubs, schools, 'dining rooms', and so on. Much of this community was destroyed by the local authority in the 1960s and 1970s because it was felt people should not live near such a heavily industrialised marshland area.

OWNERSHIP OF THE MARSH

After 1700, although some plots of land were in private hands, most of the area was owned by large charities. They could afford to take a long term and detached view and, as we shall see, they were very important in determining how the marsh developed.

The Boreman Charity

At the Restoration of Charles II, after the English Civil War, a large parcel of land was granted to a Sir William Boreman by the King. Some of it was sold by his widow but the remainder went to help pay for a charity school which Boreman had founded in Greenwich.

This charity was, and is still, administered by the Worshipful Company of Drapers in the City of London. The remaining marshland was sold in the 1870s - but decisions taken by the Drapers Company's on land management still have an effect.

Trinity Hospital

On the Greenwich riverfront, near the London Underground Power Station, is a little 'Strawberry Hill Gothic' almshouse. This is another charity, often known as 'Trinity Hospital', which dates from 1613, and is administered by the Worshipful Company of Mercers in the City of London. 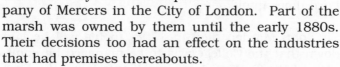 Part of the marsh was owned by them until the early 1880s. Their decisions too had an effect on the industries that had premises thereabouts.

The Poor of Farningham & Hatcliffe's Charity

A few fields were administered for the benefit of poor people in the parish of Farningham in Kent. This was land left by a benefactor, who was probably one of the Roper family.

Another piece of land was owned by Hatcliffe's Charity - whose almshouses still stand in Tuskar Street in Greenwich and resulted from a Jacobean bequest.

Morden College

The land which Boreman's widow sold in 1698 was bought by a merchant, Sir John Morden. He used it to endow Morden College, one of the most important, but least known, institutions in Greenwich.

John Roque's map of London, published in 1744, shows Greenwich Marsh and Blackwall Lane. South of it is the open space of Blackheath and on the far side is a large square building built around a quadrangle and marked 'Morden College'. These buildings, shown on the eighteenth century map, are just the same today. So many modern institutional buildings are in the Wren style that it is sometimes difficult to take in that sometimes you are looking at the real thing. The only change is that the 'decayed Turkey merchants', for whom it was set up, are now in short supply and the charity houses, in accordance with its charter, those who have fallen on hard times in old age.

Sir John Morden died in 1708. In his will he laid down that the College was to be managed by nominees of the Turkey Company, if this failed the East India Company, and on their demise the Court of Aldermen of the City of London. This succession has duly proceeded. Should be the City Corporation be abolished Sir John's requirement in his will is that future management should be by 'seven discreet and grave Gentlemen of Kent'.

Throughout the nineteenth century the Chairmen of Morden College's trustees were bankers – often members of the Lubbock family, who were based in Farnborough, Kent. Another long serving member was Thomas Baring, a banker with extensive landholdings in neighbouring Lewisham. The trustees did the best they could, in the light of their experiences as financiers, to maximise land values for the good of the charity with which they were entrusted. It was a careful, and responsible, trusteeship and their successors continue with this charge today.

A view of the Naval College from Greenwich Marsh, c.1825. Reproduced by kind permission of the London Borough of Greenwich.

These grandees were members of a 'charmed circle'[3]- the small world at the top of London banking where vast empires were controlled from a City Office.

Much of the pattern of Greenwich marsh's future was shaped by Morden College, and its surveyors. They were concerned with building standards and the type of activity to be allowed on their sites. For a period in the nineteenth century the same man, George Smith, held the position of surveyor to both Morden College and the Mercers' Company and, as will be seen, he played a key role in the marsh's development.

THE NATURAL WORLD

Greenwich marsh has not been 'natural' for many hundreds of years - if indeed it ever was. It became man-made when the River was kept out of it and the land has been managed from the time it was reclaimed from the River. When human economic activity in this area moved away from farming into what we think of as industry, then factories were built on the marsh to replace agriculture.

The land has been used for the economic benefit of those who did not live there. The area has been shaped by people, many of whom were bankers in the City of London - had probably never seen it.

2. EARLY INDUSTRY ON THE MARSH

Industry came surprisingly slowly to Greenwich Marsh – despite the fact that Greenwich itself was a bustling manufacturing town from at least Tudor times. Early industrial development spread from two areas – a settlement at the end of the road now known as Riverway and from Enderby Wharf. Much of the central area of the marsh retained a rural character into the late nineteenth century. There is even a photograph of a small haystack that dates from the 1920s!

'Rural industry' is a commercial activity and it is different to subsistence farming. Such activity was undertaken on Greenwich Marsh. Morden College records show that, although some fields were let to the tenants of surrounding farms, many who grazed cattle and sheep on the marsh were 'butchers' who kept stock on a short-term basis before sending it to market. One leaseholder was a 'basket maker' growing reeds and willow as a cash crop – a typical commercial use. Marshlands have a particular economy of their own and meant eel traps and wild fowling alongside grazing and reed beds. Before 1800 the Thames supported a major fishing industry and Greenwich was one of the main ports for fish sent to market in London. 'Watermen' used the marshland - one was evicted from his landing place for unknown reasons in 1694. The River provided a means of transport – and this is the main reason why no effective road system developed until the twentieth century. In 1803 some workers were injured in a boiler explosion at the end of Riverway* - and a wherry was called which could quickly take them to St.Thomas' Hospital by London Bridge – a clear example of how the all-encompassing River was the natural form of transport.

RURAL INDUSTRIES

Some elements of a rural economy were to remain on Greenwich marsh for many years. Throughout the early nineteenth century fields were let to a Mr.Wheatley, who ran a local horse omnibus service – a reminder that the factories described were surrounded by meadows used for grazing. Wheatley had run a major network of routes but by the 1860s was reduced to plying between the local railway stations. Nevertheless there were horses to feed and throughout the nineteenth century Wheatley could be found renting meadows from Morden College.

THE GOVERNMENT MAGAZINE

At the end of the seventeenth century a large building,

---

* See Chapter 3 'Richard Trevithick'

by any definition 'industrial', was established on the west bank of the marsh. This was a Crown establishment and it marks a change in the way the Marsh was exploited.

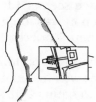

The Royal Palace in Greenwich had been the site of arms manufacture since Tudor times. The foundation of these arms establishments was a process that accelerated after the English Civil War. In Tudor times Greenwich armour was world famous, and on the Lewisham borders stood the 'armoury mill' which later produced small arms.

Work on ammunition was carried out in the Tilt Yard at the Palace and later moved to Woolwich to become, in due course, the Royal Arsenal. Greenwich lay between the two Royal Dockyards at Woolwich and Deptford - both producing warships in need of guns and ammunition.

GUNPOWDER

A complementary activity to armaments manufacture was the storage and distribution of gunpowder. Up until the seventeenth century the Ordnance Office stored this in the Tower of London. In 1694 the Principal Officers to the Office told the Treasury that they needed money for a new 'Powderhouse' somewhere convenient where gunpowder could be delivered by the manufacturers, then tested and distributed as required. What was needed was a remote riverside site near London, and the area of Greenwich marsh must have seemed ideal. The site chosen for the gunpowder depot was on the West Bank of the Marsh - near where Enderby House stands today.

The main building was a 'proof house' where gunpowder was tested for quality. This was large, featureless, and square. It was built of brick at an estimated cost of £2,306 15s. It was almost windowless and must have looked very grim from outside. The gunpowder was protected from damp by special arrangements inside, perhaps an internal false wall. There were two wings - one with a chimney - and there was a spire on the roof for venting the controlled explosions during testing.

Gunpowder was made in privately owned mills throughout the south east of England – in the Lea Valley at Sewardstone and Enfield, on the Thames at Bedfont, south of London at Chilworth, and Wimbledon, and down river at Faversham. It was transported to the Greenwich magazine by water – for reasons of both convenience and safety. Supplies were then sent to naval depots at Portsmouth, Chatham, Woolwich, and so on, as well as to garrisons around the country and naval bases as far away as Minorca, Antigua, Jamaica and Nova Scotia.

The use of water transport meant that wharfage arrangements at the riverside were most important - it would be a very busy area with some large vessels calling. The wharf itself was known as 'the bridge' and there were two pairs of gates to the waterside from the factory.

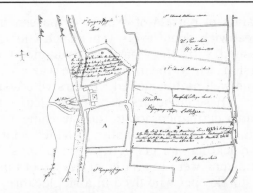

Plan of the Government Magazine. Kind permission of the Trustees of the Martin Collection.

The Powder Magazine near Greenwich 1794. Despite this date (shown on the print) it is likely to have been drawn at least twenty years earlier. Reproduced by kind permission of London Borough of Greenwich

Thousands of barrels of explosives passed through
the Greenwich depot every year. Each consignment
was issued with the Board of Ordnance's written
permission, which meant that there was an army of
clerks as well as the skilled workers who tested the
powder. These labourers were all 'settled' - that is,
they had a permanent job in the government service.
They had to wear specially provided clothing -
'calfskin leather aprons' and 'worn pumps'. Two
'proofmasters' were in charge of the depot and there
was a storekeeper who lived in a single storey building on site. In 1754 his name was Robert Furnis.

LOCAL OBJECTIONS

Not surprisingly Greenwich residents did not appre-
ciate the presence of this large store of explosives on
their doorsteps. In 1718 and again in 1750 they
petitioned Parliament to have it removed.

*"Reason for removing the Magazine of Gunpowder
at Greenwich to some more convenient place and
further Distance from the said Town and the Cities
of London and Westminster.
The apparent Danger the said Magazine is exposed
to, of being blown up by Treachery, lightning and
other Accidents, arising from its present defence-
less Situation and ruinous condition, and the extensive and scarce repairable Damage with which the
Explosion of perhaps 6 or 8,000 barrels of powder
must be attended, cannot but cause terrible appre-
hensions to all who seriously consider it.*[4]

Eventually, four Government inspectors decided that
the Greenwich Depot did indeed present a risk and

recommended that it should be moved to Purfleet. The last powder was delivered in 1768 and the depot closed soon after. The entire workforce went to Purfleet except for a Robert Dyer, who was old and ill and so retired with a pension.

What happened to the buildings after they were closed? The Government inspectors had said that they were 'improperly and dangerously situated' and 'utterly incapable of being effectually repaired' and they appear to have been demolished in 1770. Thirty years later the site was apparently sold, to Henry Vansittart - a Vice-Admiral and father of the future Lord Bexley. [5]

There was an echo of the public disquiet about the works in 1815 when a private gunpowder magazine was planned in Charlton. A petition was quickly put together pointing out the fears that local people had had about the old magazine.

In 1846 a pub in Eastney Street was burnt to the ground. It was a dreadful fire - a bedridden old lady was only rescued through the 'bold daring of a young sailor.'[6] The pub's name was the 'Royal Magazine' – evidence that the Gunpowder Depot was remembered, if only by Greenwich drinkers.

AN EARLY CHEMICAL INDUSTRY

As the eighteenth century progressed there were signs of the arrival of new industries. There may have been a bleaching business before 1770 at Dog Kennel Field, described as a 'Whiters House and Garden'. This probably meant it was used for the bleaching of paper or cloth. If so it was in effect the

the first commercial industrial premises on the marsh. Seventy years later a 'bleaching house' appears on a deed covering an area at the western end of Bendish Marsh. Maybe it had some connection with the Enderby family's ropewalk.

Traditional bleaching methods needed space and water. There were flourishing bleach fields close by Greenwich – north of the Thames in the Lea Valley and east along the Darenth Valley. Samuel Parkes, a writer on chemistry who knew east London well, commented in 1839 that from around 1750 sulphuric acid began to be used in bleaching processes.[7] In this context it should be noted that there may also have been a vitriol - sulphuric acid - factory established nearby.

A Perspective view of the River Thames etc. taken from the Kings Arms at Blackwall. There is a tiny gibbet on the riverside on the right of the picture. Reproduced by kind permission of London Borough of Greenwich.

3. THE EAST BANK

MR BUGSBY

The east bank of the Peninsula was developed soon
after the Gunpowder Depot had closed. This stretch
of the River is called 'Bugsby's Reach'. The name
probably dates from the early eighteenth century.
Earlier it was called Cockle's Reach or Podd's Elms
Reach. The 1744 Roque map shows a great semi
circle of trees stretching across both sides of Horn
Lane - which must have been a memorable sight
from the River. Perhaps it was when the trees died
or were felled that the name was changed.

The end of Riverway, then called Marsh Lane, was
known as 'Bugsby's Hole'. 'Hole' is a term used along
the Thames, and means a deep part of the riverbed
where shipping could lie in safety. Bugsby seems to
be someone's name. Who was he? There was no
major landowner or a tenant with that name here in
the eighteenth century. One story is that Bugsby
was a robber who hid himself and his swag in an
osier bed here.

GIBBETS

It has been suggested that the word 'Bugsby' has something to do with bogeys and bugaboos.[8] This is because it is possible that Bugsby's Hole was used as a site for gibbeting the bodies of pirates who had been hung, with due ceremony, at Execution Dock in Wapping. How many such horrible exhibitions took place is not clear but 'Williams' was gibbeted here in 1735. When such gibbets were used some security arrangements were necessary because relations of gibbeted criminals naturally tried to reclaim the bodies - pirates had families like everyone else. Was this why there was a watch house on the Marsh?

Gibbeting didn't stop piracy and in 1816 a robbery took place, described as *'one of the greatest robberies ever to have taken place in this country'*[9] This involved the theft of £13,000 in dollars, from the hoy, *Coromandel*, which was transferring it to another ship bound for India. The pirates were caught because they left some of the chests full of money lying on the foreshore. Perhaps they are the men who were gibbeted below Blackwall Point in 1816. If so, they are just another part of the grisly history of this area.

On the north bank of the River at Blackwall a large shipbuilding and ship repair depot was in use. This belonged to the powerful East India Company and all the riverside activities on Greenwich marsh from the eighteenth century onwards took place to a background of the movements of the great ships owned by the Company. East Indiamen sailed to the far corners of the earth to exploit what they found there. To many of the remote people they visited they must have seemed like the alien spacecraft we imagine today – so high-tech that their possibilities could only just be grasped. To Greenwich people they were a sign that the whole world could be grasped by those with enough capital and the right technology.

NEW EAST GREENWICH

In Riverway stands one of the few remains of early nineteenth century industry in Greenwich - The Pilot pub. A plaque - which might be of any date - reads *'New East Greenwich, 1804'*.

In 1804 the site's owner was George Russell who was a very successful soapmaker. Beginning from very little he had built up the Old Bargehouse soapworks at Blackfriars until it became the largest soap factory in England. He was involved in many activities - and owned many parcels of land, in London, Kent and Ireland. He owned two coal transport ships – colliers - called *Nymph* and *Russell*. It may be that he also had a riverside house in Greenwich because in 1796 he was burgled by a gang of thieves who escaped by boat. His main residence was a big house at Longlands near Sidcup in Kent. In 1792 he had bought some land on the east bank of the Greenwich Peninsula. It was used to make bricks, which were probably sold for the many building developments going on in Greenwich at the time.

In the 1790s Russell's brickmakers made a hole in the sea wall without permission. Philip Sharpe, the Wall Reeve (a local official) visited the site where he met Russell's agent, Thomas Taylor. In reply to his questions Taylor said *'Damn your eyes, Mr. Sharp, if you come here I will poke your teeth and stop your eyes with mud'* and then he told a bystander, John Bignall, to throw Sharpe off the wall'.[10] Which Bignell proceeded to do.   Nothing very much seems to have happened to either Taylor or Bignell for this act of violence – within a year Bignell had got Sharpe's job as Wall Reeve.

WILLIAM PITT

In 1801 part of the site was re-leased to a consortium which included William Pitt, who had recently resigned as Prime Minister. It also involved Pitt's elder brother, Lord North, and a local landowner, the Hon. John Eliot and his brother. They were all members of the Privy Council, all out of office and related to each other. What exactly did these four elite politicians want with this obscure piece of riverside?   We may never know but it is likely that they wanted to invest in a new venture being undertaken there.   It is possible that this was a scheme known as the London Flour Company.

It is usually assumed that 'The Pilot' - the name of the pub in Riverway - refers to pilots who worked on the River but there is a good case to be made out that it derives from a song about William Pitt.

'When our perils are past, shall our gratitude sleep?
No, - here's to the pilot that weathered the storm."[11]

These verses were composed by George Canning, the future Prime Minister, and sung by a popular tenor, Charles Dignum, at a dinner on Pitt's birthday in 1802. The Treaty of Amiens had been signed two

IMPORTANT

FREEHOLD ESTATE,

LAND TAX REDEEMED.

Particulars and Conditions of Sale,

OF A SPACIOUS BRICK-BUILT

TIDE FLOUR MILL,

WITH SLATED ROOF,

SITUATE ON THE BANK OF THE THAMES, AT EAST GREENWICH, KENT,

WITH

EXTENSIVE PONDS TO SUPPLY THE MILL,

THE FRONTAGE NEXT THE RIVER

IS ABOUT

1200 FEET,

Which renders the Property valuable for the purpose of Erecting

EXTENSIVE MANUFACTORIES,

OR FOR

SHIP BUILDERS' YARDS OR DOCKS.

A CAPITAL RESIDENCE,

WITH PLEASURE GROUNDS AND GARDENS,

STABLING AND OUT HOUSES,

THE "PILOT," PUBLIC HOUSE,

Seventeen Brick Dwelling Houses,

In Ceylon Place, near the Residence.

Which will be Sold by Auction,

BY

SOUTHEY AND SON,

At the Auction Mart, Bartholomew Lane,

On THURSDAY, the 16th Day of JUNE, 1842, at Twelve o'Clock,

May be Viewed till the Sale, and Particulars had upon the Premises ; at the Ship & Billet, Woolwich Road ; Prince of Orange, Greenwich ; of Messrs. BRIDGES & MASON, Solicitors, Red Lion Square, Holborn ; of Messrs. ASTON & WALLIS, Solicitors, 2, New Broad Street ; of Mr. SUTER, Surveyor, Fenchurch Street ; at Garraway's, and of SOUTHEY & SON, 191, Tooley Street

Advertisement for the sale of the East Greenwich Tide Mill in 1842.

months earlier and one of the clauses put Ceylon under the protection of the British Crown - hence 'Ceylon Place', which is the name of the cottages.

THE TIDE MILL

In 1800 steam engines were becoming an ever-present reality and the future of industrial power was with them. In the meantime the heaviest industrial muscle was that provided by the power of the tide. The biggest installations on the Thames were tide mills.

William Johnson had patented a tide mill design in 1801. In 1802 he approached Morden College and asked if he could lease a site for 'a water corn mill' - a tide mill with a wheel which could be adjusted to the ebb and flow of the tide. They refused and he then approached the Court of Sewers for permission to open the riverbank and later the City of London Commissioners, who were in charge of the Riverbank

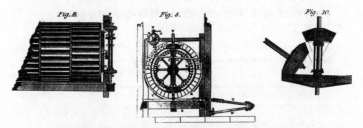

Mill machinery at East Greenwich, from Olinthus Gregory, 'Mechanics'. Part of the equipment used in the machinery of the mill wheel at East Greenwich. Fig 5 is a section of the water wheel, Fig 6.is a part of the water wheel, and Fig.10 dressing equipment suggested by the Foreman of the mill works.

itself. While they were happy with his plans, the Greenwich Court was not and an argument ensued. By then Johnson was in discussion with George Russell.

By 1803 the mill was under construction on the riverside site adjacent to The Pilot and Ceylon Place. Is it possible that the pits from which Russell's workers had dug the brick earth were used for the four acres of ponds, which were soon to be constructed behind the mill? Parts of these ponds were to last well into the twentieth century.

One afternoon, in 1802, Olinthus Gregory, Professor of Mathematics at the Royal Military Academy in Woolwich, went for a riverside walk. He stopped for a chat with the foreman on the mill site; and later wrote an account of what he had seen there. The mill being built was to stand parallel to the Thames with a channel under it. This allowed river water to flow in and fill the ponds behind it with water on the incoming tide. The mill wheel stood in this channel and worked as the tide came in. When the tide went out it reversed and the water in the millponds behind was released - so that it could work continuously.

A lot of money must have been invested in the mill and it was constructed by a leading millwright of the day. This was John Lloyd who also building the Government armaments establishment at Waltham Abbey. Lloyd knew about steam engines and used them where they would be useful to him. At East Greenwich a steam engine was used in construction work - and this led to the mill site becoming famous.

RICHARD TREVITHICK

Richard Trevithick, the 'Cornish giant' is one of the pioneers of steam engine development. In 1803 he came to London to promote sales of a new sort of engine. George Russell ordered an eight horsepower high pressure engine from him. The engine had a round boiler seated above a fire enclosed inside a brick box. There was also a safety valve to let excess steam off into the open air and so prevent accidents.

The steam engine was used to pump water out from the foundations of the new mill. On Thursday, 8th September 1803, a boy, who had been left in charge of the engine was told to go and catch eels. First, he fastened the safety lever down and wedged it tight with a piece of wood. The result was inevitable - the boiler burst *'with an explosion as sudden and as dreadful as a powder mill'*[12] One piece of boiler, an inch thick and weighing 5 cwt, was thrown 125 yards in the air and *'landing on the ground made a hole eighteen inches deep'.*[13] Bricks were thrown in a *'circle of two hundred feet, no two of them stayed together'.*[14] Three men were killed and three more injured. One, Thomas Naylor who had been covered in boiling water, died a week later in St.Thomas's Hospital. Another was deafened, but, like the boy, was soon back at work. The newspapers were quick to report the accident and it was then taken up by rival steam engine manufacturers, Boulton and Watt. Later, Trevithick was to say that *'Boulton and Watt are about to do me every injury in their power .. they have done their best to report the explosion both in the newspapers and in private letters very different to what it really was'.*[15] A week later the Times commented that Mr. Watt's engines would not explode in this way.

Others in the press said that the incident should be a *'warning to engineers to construct their safety valves so that common workmen cannot stop them at their pleasure'.*[16] In future Trevithick's boilers had more than one safety vent.

The accident is recounted in almost every account of Trevithick and the steam engine. It had a great deal of influence for many years – perhaps the history of the steam engine would be different if it had not happened.

Mr. Trevithick's High Pressure Engine. From Farey, 'Treatise on the Steam Engine'.

THE MILL IN USE

The mill was first operated for two or three years by William Johnson. There are no records as to why he left or if it was a success. He went on to have a distinguished engineering career.

After Johnson a number of other millers worked at East Greenwich. George Russell had died in 1804 and the mill became the subject of a lengthy Chancery case. Ultimately the freehold appears to have continued with his son, another George, and in some directories 'George Russell' is given as the miller. More often it was whoever was currently actually operating the mill – as with a Mr. Doust who paid rates for some years. The most frequently mentioned was Thomas Pattrick - indeed it was sometimes known as 'Pattrick's Mill'.

It seems likely, however, that the mill was never a real success and was eventually advertised for sale in June 1842. It was bought by a Frank Hills, and as soon as it was sold he hurried to the Court of Sewers demanding a rate reduction. He said that it had not been used for years and was very dilapidated - it was, in fact, just a *stack of materials*.[17] He got his rate reduction so perhaps there was some truth in what he said.

What Frank Hills did with the mill belongs to another chapter but it survived him and was still there, with its wheels and everything intact when he died in the 1890s. By the 1920s the buildings had gone but some of the ponds remained, crossed by a boardwalk.

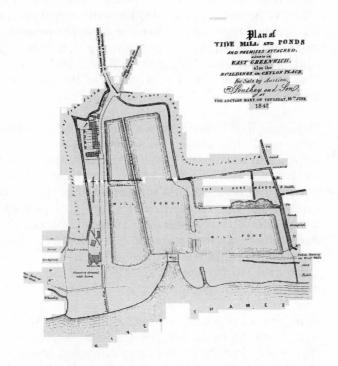

Plan of Tide Mill and the surrounding area drawn when the mill was put up for sale in 1842

NEW EAST GREENWICH

'New East Greenwich' was never really more than a street of houses surrounded by some very dirty industry. The inhabitants were the first permanent residents on the Marsh - a community that was to grow and flourish over the next hundred and fifty years. Today only the oldest cottages and the pub are still there.

It may be that these were not the first buildings in this area and this leads to another mystery. A house appears to have been built, perhaps at the same time as the mill, and was later called East Lodge. There are several unsubstantiated stories of a structure under East Lodge - of vaulted cellars and of a passageway which led out towards the road. The house was demolished at the start of the twentieth century, Greenwich Yacht Club were on this site for many years but no investigations have ever been done to show what have been there.

A notorious resident of East Lodge was a Mr. Hewes who lived there in the 1840s and is said to have disrupted church services by sitting on the upstairs window ledge and playing the trumpet. He used it as a 'house of pleasure'.

East Lodge became an island of peace in the middle of an increasingly dirty and oppressive industrial area. In the middle of the nineteenth century the daughters of the chemical work's manager lived there and remembered their riverside home as a place of beauty and happiness.

East Lodge – the big house on the riverside at Greenwich Marsh - from a painting by Dora Sainsbury. Reproduced by kind permission Maj Wagstaff

4.ENDERBY WHARF AND THE ENDERBY FAMILY

ENDERBY WHARF

The first factory to be built on the Greenwich Peninsula stood on the site of the seventeenth century gunpowder depot. Since then the site has been in almost continuous occupation - and, in effect, in the same ownership. Items made there have had worldwide importance. It is still known by the name of a family who used it over 150 years ago - Enderby Wharf. Beside it on the riverbank stands their home, Enderby House.

VITRIOL AND COPPERAS

The gunpowder depot buildings must have stood unused for many years until, around 1800, George Moor opened a 'vitriol' works on 'Crown Land'. It is very likely that 'Crown Land' refers to the old government gunpowder depot – by then unused. George Moor (or Moore) was most probably a copperas manufacturer who was using this as a raw material for the manufacture of vitriol (sulphuric acid). Copperas works had been found on the Thames estuary since mediaeval times. It was made from pyrites or 'copperas stones', which were picked up on the beaches of the Thames Estuary and then steeped in tanks of water for several years. A liquor was produced which could be used to make dyes, mordents or processed for more sophisticated chemicals.

The Deptford copperas works, opened by Sir Nicholas Crispe, was described to the Royal Society in 1678. There were more works on the east bank of the Ravensbourne (Deptford Creek) in Greenwich - one of which had been associated with a Mr. Moore. From the 1730s Thomas Moore had been in occupation of Coombe Farm (near today's Westcombe Park Station) and it is possible that he and George Moore were related. After 1800 a George Moor was to take on leases for several areas of Greenwich Marsh. The vitriol works on Greenwich Marsh did not necessarily make acid by traditional methods using copperas, but could have used the 'chamber process'. This had been developed about fifty years previously under conditions of great secrecy. A list drawn up by a chemist many years later mentions seven such works in London, but Moore is not included. Several new industries, including copperas, had been developed in Greenwich following the Civil War. Some historians have pointed out that a chemical industry needed to be in place as a forerunner to the industrial revolution.[18] Greenwich was thus well placed to be in the forefront of new industrial developments.

The vitriol works may have had some connection with the bleaching house mentioned above. It might also have had some investment or impetus from Henry Vansittart who is said to have bought the Government Magazine site and also had some connection with the bleaching business. Vansittart was a much travelled Admiral and explorer – and, in 1803, brother to the Chancellor of the Exchequer. The family had strong local links both in Greenwich and the immediate Kent countryside – and with some of the grandees who lived in Greenwich, Blackheath and beyond.

ROPE

The vitriol works was still in place on the Peninsula thirty years later, but owned by a Lewis Price. Meanwhile a Mr. Littlewood had opened a ropewalk nearby. This ropewalk connects Greenwich with one of the most successful ironfounders of the late seventeenth century. Ambrose Crowley III had come to Greenwich in 1704 with a successful business as an iron founder in both the Midlands and North East England. In 1782, because there was no Crowley heir, a partnership was set up which included Isaiah Millington who had been Crowley's salaried Manager. By the early nineteenth century the Millingtons were the leading industrial family in Greenwich with strong links to the Pearsons, who owned copperas works throughout the Thameside area. The ropewalk was developed by the Millingtons in partnership with an otherwise unidentified Mr. Young. Thus it was an investment by the leading Greenwich industrialist of the day.

Rope making is sometimes thought of as a very traditional kind of manufacture. Around 1800 it was one of the many processes which were undergoing change and improvement. There was an increasing need for more and better rope – for all the great ships in the navy and the merchant marine. Joseph Huddart had set up a factory in Limehouse to make rope by a revolutionary new method and it may be that some of his ideas were used in Greenwich. Rope is made in long narrow buildings called 'rope walks'. The ropewalk at Enderby Wharf remained in place for nearly a century and the shape of it can be seen by looking inland from the riverside path through the gates to the Alcatel works. It was slightly to the left of the long path which goes down through the centre of the factory buildings.

By the late 1830s the Enderby family had acquired the ropewalk. They had a number of industrial interests but are best known as whalers. Their ships went all round the world and their Greenwich works made the sort of items sold by ships chandlers – rope, sacking and so on. Greenwich was also home to a whaling fleet.

HUNTING THE WHALE

In 1814 Samuel Enderby had an 'oil and white lead' works in Loman Street, in The Borough, Southwark. Earlier family members had been involved in a tannery in Bermondsey - the national centre for the tanning industry. Samuel Enderby had helped pioneer a process to make white lead in which tannery waste was an important ingredient. He was also in the 'oil and Russia' trade, which probably meant that he processed mutton fat imported from the Baltic together with oil from whales slaughtered by the crews of his ships. He owned an oil processing plant at Rotherhithe, where oil, removed at sea from the dead whales, was dealt with. Oil had all sorts of uses but, in the days before coal gas, was often used for street lighting.

Mary Buxton's family were ship owners and when she married a Samuel Enderby he took over her family business. Their ships were among those chartered to take tea cargoes to Boston, Massachusetts – with obvious links to the earliest days of American independence. Samuel's ships went out to hunt sperm whale and by 1790 he was a rich man controlling sixty-eight whaling ships working in the Southern Oceans. These ships began to set new standards of success - an Enderby crew were the first to harpoon a whale in the Pacific and one of his ships was the first to round the Horn with a cargo of sperm whale oil. Two hundred years ago this was considered heroic and the crews of the ships and the Enderby family gained a great deal of respect.

THE ENDERBY FAMILY AND THEIR HOME

Until 1830 the Enderby business headquarters was at St. Paul's Wharf in the City of London. Later they moved away from the riverside to Great St.Helens, near Bishopsgate but by this time Samuel's sons were in charge. The family was very numerous but the best known after the two Samuels, father and son, are grandsons, Charles and George. A later family member with Greenwich connections was Charles 'Chinese' Gordon.

The Enderby family had lived in Greenwich for a long time before they opened their riverside factory. In the 1790s Samuel, Jnr. had occupied a large and impressive house on Crooms Hill. His mother lived on Blackheath and was involved in a long argument with Morden College about her tenancy. Family members were active in local good causes. Elizabeth Enderby - wife of another brother - opened a School for Orphan Girls in Royal Hill; George Enderby was patron of a local savings bank; several of the family subscribed to St. Mary's church, which was built in 1823 near the southwest gates of Greenwich Park.

Once the Enderby brothers bought the Greenwich riverside site Charles and George Enderby are said to have lived there. Perhaps they did so because of the wonderful riverside views since there could have been no need for people so rich and successful to live in this remote and marshy location. Enderby

Enderby House built in the 1840s, the house stands on the Greenwich riverside and is now used as offices by Alcatel. Reproduced by kind permission of Sally Jenkinson

House, which still stands on the riverside, was probably built in the 1840s and replaced other houses which had been burnt down. Charles entertained the rich and famous here. He had a number of 'curiosities' including a Tudor bedstead and a stuffed 'parson bird' from New Zealand, which, when alive, had been a pet. Enderby House is now used as offices and is not accessible to visitors. It contains some beautiful and unusual rooms '*an octagonal room. Large bay window, elegant pilasters, heavily decorated cornice and glass domed roof*'[19]

THE RIVERSIDE FACTORY

The Enderby's factory consisted of two large waterside buildings where spinning machinery and looms were used to make canvas. There were also rooms where hemp was spun and a flax mill on site.   Outdoors were buildings to house a steam engine and boiler, houses for the foremen, stables, a smithy, and a joinery.

A feature of the factory was a 'pitch house'. Experiments had been carried out in the Naval Dockyards with coal tar – produced by the new gas industry - for ropemaking. At first Royal Dockyard workers had refused to handle it because of the smell but it was probably used here by the Enderbys' workers. The brothers negotiated seven-year contracts with the gas companies for a supply of tar and there was also a project with the City of London Gas Company for making 'composition'. This most often means a coal tar based mortar used by the cheaper end of the building trade and something that was to be made by other east Greenwich manufacturers in due course.

The brothers also maintained their whaling interests. Their most famous ship was built on the Isle of Wight – and called the 'Samuel Enderby'. A picture of it hangs in Enderby House. For her first voyage an experimental rot proofing was used. This was Kyan's extremely poisonous sublimate solution - more usually used as a treatment for syphilis. As a result there was some nausea among those who worked on her.

Such uses of chemical products still under development in the 1830s shows how close the Enderby brothers were to many of the new ideas about chemistry and its development at that time.

THE FIRST TELEGRAPH CABLES

In 1837 the Enderby brothers were approached by William Cooke, the pioneer inventor of the telegraph, who asked for help in developing a specially insulated rope. This was for the earliest experiments in setting up the electric telegraph in which Cooke wanted to establish an electric telegraph across the Thames. It was possibly this cable that was used in the first trials of the telegraph on the railway up Camden Bank between Euston and Camden Town.[20] If so, this means that the earliest effective telegraph cable was made in Greenwich. Later owners of the site made cables that stretched across the world and in so doing followed on work already done by the Enderby family.

A NEW WORLD

A younger generation of Enderbys had money and leisure. Charles was to be one of the founders of the Royal Geographical Society and used his ships for exploration – something that also helped his whaling interests. Enderby ships became identified with Antarctic exploration and the stories of the explorers with their, sometimes harrowing, adventures make exciting reading. They named the new lands which they discovered 'Adelaide Island' after Queen Adelaide, 'Mount William', after William IV - and, of course, 'Enderby Land'.

The Enderbys were part of that circle of merchants with strong government and establishment links - the same people who ran Morden College and the East India Company. Exploration was an expensive business: in theory, it was undertaken to discover new areas for whale fishing but this trade was soon in decline. In 1847 Charles Enderby got a concession to set up a whaling station in the Auckland Islands in Antarctica - the 'Southern Whale Fishery'. It was a short lived and unsuccessful venture in which he, and the other members of his family, lost a lot of money.

THE FIRE

In 1845 the Enderbys planned to extend the Green- wich works by building right up to the river's edge. Before the work began a serious fire left the works in ruins. The factory's own fire engine fought the blaze joined by two from the Parish, another from the Royal Dockyard and one from the London Fire

Brigade Establishment. A detachment of Royal
Marines was sent to help but there was never very
much hope of saving the ropewalk.   By the next
morning all that remained were the '*lofty walls*' of the
factory - and they were blown down by the high
winds in the next few days.   It was said in the
Kentish Mercury that the fire was either
'*spontaneous combustion*' or that it was   '*wilfully
raised by some incendiary*'.

Work on a replacement building seems to have
begun but was probably never finished.   Charles
Enderby seems to have continued to live on site until
about 1849.   The future was to be much more
exciting.

*Fire at East Greenwich. The Enderby Bros. Works
burns down in 1845. From a contemporary Illustrated
London News*

5. THE ATLANTIC CABLE

Enderby Wharf has been identified with the laying of the Atlantic Cable. However, the story starts on a site a few hundred yards further north - Morden Wharf. In the 1830s Morden College began to parcel out sites to those who were willing to develop them and a large site, including both that now covered by the Amylum Works as well as the area of Morden Wharf, was let to a Charles Holcombe. He began to sub-let areas within this site to 'suitable' industrial tenants. One of these was a cable maker, William Kuper.

KUPER AND CABLES

The story of the development and laying of telegraph cables is complicated and involves many people and companies. This account is limited to the aspects relevant to cable manufacture in Greenwich. In the early 1850s technology was sufficiently far advanced to lay a telegraph cable between England and France. Cable making itself had been developed by a number of inventors working for different manufacturers. In particular, the use of gutta percha, a rubber like substance obtained from trees in Malaya and only recently discovered, had been developed by a specialist firm – The Gutta Percha Company. Most of the development work had been done in east and north east London - not, as yet, in Greenwich, despite the work done by the Enderbys. The first cables were made of twisted wires in a similar way to the 'wire rope', used for haulage in mines and quarries. An early manufacturer of wire rope, and later cable, was William Kuper and Co. whose works was alongside the Surrey Canal in Camberwell.

Cable manufacture was still in its early stages and before undersea cables could be made considerable difficulties had to be overcome - the first attempts were not a success. Kuper received some of the sub-contract work for the second attempt and, since it was successful, more orders followed.

GLASS ELLIOTT

George Elliott was a mining engineer working for the Marquis of Londonderry whose pits in the Durham coalfield were a major supplier of coal to Greenwich industries. He had worked in an advisory capacity at Newall's at whose Gateshead cable works most of the telegraph cables laid up to then had been made. Elliott became Kuper's agent and could provide the expertise to make the company financially viable and at the same time help them move to a new Greenwich factory, at Morden Wharf East. They took

Sir Richard Glass. From 'Illustrated London News'

George Elliott. From 'Newcastle Worthies'.

possession of a new building which Holcombe had erected, of a *sound and substantial character* as Morden College had specified.

Soon after moving to Greenwich, Elliott took over Kuper's completely together with Richard Attwood Glass - they called the new firm Glass Elliott. Elliott went on to become MP for Newcastle, and Glass became Secretary of the Stock Exchange. At Morden Wharf their first commission was to make the cable for a submarine link between Northern Italy and Corsica and for this they made sheathing to cover a core already made by the Gutta Percha Company at Wharf Road in Islington.

The manufacture of this Italian cable was a success and it was laid under the sea by the SS *Persian*. The next cable was destined for a link across the Cabot Strait in America. Problems were encountered in loading the cable onto the ship from Morden Wharf and, to deal with this, cable pits were dug in which the cable was coiled up and tested underwater while it was still in storage.

MORDEN WHARF

Contemporary drawings show the works at Morden Wharf with 'Glass Elliot, Submarine Cables' written on the roof of the main buildings, at an angle so as to be seen from the River. They also show two pits lined with bricks, and a bridge in-between with arched drainage ducts underneath. From these coiled cables could be loaded on to the ship. While techniques for handling the cable were perfected, survey work went on for the laying of the Atlantic Telegraph cable. For this a new company - The

The Atlantic Cable, ready for shipment at Morden Wharf, East Greenwich. Note the special circular tanks in which the cable was coiled. From 'Illustrated London News'.

Finsihing off the manufacture of the Atlantic Cable, ready for shipment at Morden Wharf, East Greenwich. From 'Illustrated London News'.

Atlantic Telegraph Company - was set up in 1856.
The provision of a telegraph link between the old and
new worlds was seen as something of paramount
importance – and there was great excitement about
it since it was recognised that overnight it could
change the way in which business and society were
organised. Interest by the public was enormous on
both sides of the Atlantic.

THE FIRST ATTEMPT AT AN ATLANTIC CABLE

The core for the first Atlantic cable was made by the
Gutta Percha Company and the job of making the
sheathing was shared between Glass Elliott, in
Greenwich, and Newall in Birkenhead. The sheathing used eighteen stranded wires woven around a
core separated by hemp soaked in tar, pitch and
linseed oil. This system is said to have been designed by Brunel and it needed enough wire to
encircle the earth three times. The cable was to be
made in 1,200 pieces, each two miles long, which
were then spliced into eight lengths of 300 miles
each. Work began on 19th December 1856. Unfortunately it turned out that the cable made in Birkenhead had a right-handed twist, while Glass Elliott,
who had thought the cable would be twisted when it
was coiled, gave theirs a left-handed twist. This, and
other problems, took time to sort out.

It was necessary to design a new method of paying
the cable out from the ships into the sea. This was
to allow control over the speed of the cable as it left
the ship, and so that it could be stowed efficiently. A

recording machine was installed on board the cable ship to check how much cable had been laid.

Half the cable was to be laid from Valentia, the westernmost point in Britain on the Irish coast and the other half from America. The Greenwich made cable went into the British ship, *Agamemnon*. She was an old '*wooden walled ship of the line*' with ninety-one guns, and had been the flagship at the bombardment of Sevastopol. That the Government lent her for the project demonstrated quite clearly the level of their backing for this apparently private project. The cable was loaded from Greenwich in July 1857 and coiled into *Agamemnon's* hold by sailors sitting on stools.

Agamemnon and the cable had a magnificent send off with a garden-party in Erith for the crew and Glass Elliot's workmen. But, despite everyone's hopes, the attempt was a failure. The cable broke in mid-Atlantic and was lost. The cable makers went back to Greenwich to start work again.

HENLEY AND ENDERBY WHARF

Glass Elliott had wanted to expand beyond Morden Wharf since 1857. Together with another cable manufacturer, W.T.Henley, they took over the Enderby site, including the ropewalk (which was to remain on site for many years to come).

In 1858 'Messrs Henley' asked the River Commissioners for permission to deepen the River so that steamers could embark and cables be loaded but Henley soon moved out to another site at North Woolwich.

Three years later Glass Elliott alone asked for permission to build a causeway at Enderby's together with another at the 'telegraph works' – still at Morden Wharf. So the long occupation of Enderby Wharf by Glass Elliott and their successors began, but for some years Morden Wharf continued to be used.

THE NEXT ATTEMPT AT LAYING AN ATLANTIC CABLE

Glass Elliott was contracted to make the cable for the second attempt in the Atlantic. Once again the cable was loaded onto *Agamemnon* and, despite many difficulties, it was successfully laid by 5th August 1858 - to rapturous acclaim in the press. Sadly the connection lasted just two months and by October nothing could be transmitted through it. Once again the cable makers returned to Greenwich and, in 1862, were ready to try again. Glass Elliott's technicians had designed a new and improved cable for the next attempt.

TELEGRAPH CONSTRUCTION AND MAINTENANCE

In April 1864 Glass Elliott merged with the Gutta Percha Company, who made the core of the new cables. This company was called the Telegraph Construction and Maintenance Co., with Sir John Pender as Chairman and with Richard Glass as Managing Director. They immediately offered to make and lay a new Atlantic cable. This time it would be more robustly constructed, heavier, and nearly double the diameter. There would be seven strands of high purity copper, six of them twisted round the seventh and there would be four layers of gutta percha. Between the copper and the gutta percha there would be a layer of resin and Stockholm Tar. As it was made, inch by inch, it was closely inspected – a break would mean another expensive disaster. The new cable was so big and heavy that Agamemnon could not carry it and it was thought three ships would be needed.

THE GREAT EASTERN

The solution came in the shape of Isambard Kingdom Brunel's enormous and unpopular ship, the *Great Eastern*. Launched seven years before from Millwall and, known as 'The Leviathan', she was designed to be bigger and more powerful than any ship before her. She had failed as a passenger liner and was thus bought very cheaply by Brunel's friend, Daniel Gooch, while he was a director of Great Western Railway Company. He promptly joined the Board of the Telegraph Construction Company and offered *Great Eastern* to them for free.

There was even greater interest in this new, third, cable and the Prince of Wales visited Greenwich to see it being manufactured. He sent a message through the 1,400 miles then being tested in the factory - '*I wish success to the Atlantic Cable*'.

Great Eastern leaving Sheerness with the Atlantic Tele-graph Cable. From 'Illustrated London News'.

Great Eastern, from W.H. Russell, 'The Atlantic Telegraph'

It took eight months to make the new cable and two weeks to load it into *Great Eastern*. The ship was so big that she could not be brought alongside Enderby Wharf and every bit of cable had to be ferried out to her. She left Greenwich for Valentia on 15th July 1865 carrying 21,000 tons dead-weight.

When they were 948 miles from Valentia and 717 miles from their destination, Heart's Content in Newfoundland, the cable was once more lost over-board. Four times the cable was found on the ocean bottom, and four times it slipped away again. Then storms set in and the cable was thought to be lost. For a while, in England, it was also believed that the Great Eastern herself had gone down - once the cable was lost no messages could be got back. Once again, the cable makers went back to Greenwich.

THE FOURTH TRY

The Telegraph Construction and Maintenance Co. made yet another new cable, which was finished in 1866.   Once again they loaded the *Great Eastern* and once again she left the Thames for Valentia. The bands on shore played '*Goodbye Sweetheart*' as she left with 2,730 miles of cable. This time, on 27th July, she reached Heart's Content and the cable was laid at last.

Great Eastern then went back to look for the broken cable lost in the previous attempt. There was no way to contact the ship once she had left but on 2nd of September instruments at the Valentia end of the broken cable began to move. Workers on board the

Great Eastern had found the broken end two miles down, brought it up, and it too was now connected. Within a few moments, both Europe and America knew where *Great Eastern* was and what she had done.   It is one of the defining moments of the modern world.

It is difficult to overstate the importance of the Atlantic cable and the *'profound transformation'* to which it led. A historian of the City of London has said that *'despite the romance of the workshop of the world ... it is in the under-publicised accounts department that the long-term future held sway'.*[21] The telegraph was a major agent of change and an instrument whose importance was not lost on City business interests, which controlled land on the Greenwich Peninsula and the companies, which made and laid the cable. The Stock Exchange was transformed by it, and by 1871 *'trading on exchanges in New York and London were effectively integrated'.*[21] Within another two years connections were made to Tokyo and Melbourne and world markets were shifting towards globalisation.

The Atlantic Telegraph Cable of 1865. Celebrations at Heart's Content, Newfoundland. From 'Illustrated London News'

At the end of the twentieth century there is much talk about the global communications revolution. The real revolution came a hundred and thirty years ago when wires twisted on Greenwich marsh crackled into life on the sea bed. It is said that for many years one of the Great Eastern's masts stood on Enderby Wharf as a reminder of what had been achieved. It was a special wooden mast that held a compass overhead above the magnetic field of the ship. It disappeared in 1965 – where is it now?

Of all the sites involved with the cable only one has an exhibition to show what happened - at Heart's Content in Newfoundland.

TELCON

There is no space here to outline all the changes in the Telegraph Construction and Maintenance Company and the Greenwich works. Between the 1870s and the present day there have, obviously, been many take-overs and structural changes. The international nature of the business can be illustrated - grimly - by the murder in 1908 of their Chief Engineer, Mr.Tom London, in Mombassa where the cable ship *Columba* had docked.

For a while the numerous cable companies made up a major Thameside industry - most are gone, but the Greenwich works remains. The need for technology for the transfer of information is as strong as ever.

Enderby House is still on the riverside. Alongside it is an office building with decorative cable and gutta percha motifs above the lintels and around the door. The wharf is no longer used, and the 'dolphins' at which the cable ships were loaded are gone. *The John W. Mackay*, a cable ship preserved there for many years has apparently now been broken up. On the jetty itself cable-loading gear still stands, unmarked, but for the moment preserved as a monument.

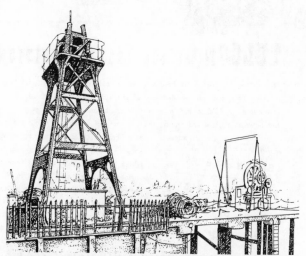

Equipment on Enderby Wharf, Greenwich. Drawing by kind permission of Sally Jenkinson. This cable loading gear is preserved on the main wharf outside Enderby House on the Greenwich Riverside Walk. Access to the jetty, and some seating, is likely to be made available.

Inside the transept of the Crystal Palace, showing the " Sibthorp " elms.

TELCON at the 1851 EXHIBITION

Telcon's founder, The Gutta Percha Company, exhibited in the Crystal Palace in Hyde Park and was awarded one of the coveted Council Medals of the Exhibition. In 1850 it had made the first submarine telegraph cable to be laid between England and France, the centenary of which was celebrated last year. From such adventurous beginnings has grown the present Telcon organisation, whose activities cover extensive fields in engineering and industry. Again, in 1951, the Festival Exhibition includes some examples of the outstanding Telcon developments of the present century.

TELCON CABLES

TELCON METALS

TELCON PLASTICS

THE TELEGRAPH CONSTRUCTION & MAINTENANCE CO. LTD
Head Office : 22 Old Broad Street, London, E.C.2.   Telephone: LONdon Wall 7104
Enquiries to : Telcon Works, Greenwich, S.E.10.   Telephone: GREenwich 3291

A 1951 advertisement for Telcon

6. COLES CHILD AND COAL

Most industrial land at East Greenwich was owned by
charities. These bodies were governed by trustees
required to maximise their income for the benefit of
the charitable institutions – responsible development
of their land was well within their remit.

The charity with the largest holding was, and is,
Morden College and in 1838 Morden College asked its
surveyor, George Smith, to evaluate their land holdings on Greenwich marsh.

DEVELOPERS

George Smith was an architect who had already been
responsible for some important buildings in Greenwich – he was Surveyor to the Cator Estate in Blackheath, and would soon be appointed as architect to
the Greenwich Railway. Crucially he was also Surveyor to the Mercer's Company – managing land
holdings on Greenwich Marsh for the Hospital of the

Blessed Trinity. Thus he represented the two largest landholders and he held these key positions over the next fifty years

Smith's work with Morden College had a very clear pattern. Sites were handed over to key tenants who 'improved' them and then sub-let to industrial users – all of whom had to be approved by Morden College. Buildings to be erected were expected to be of a high standard, and had to be approved by Smith. There was usually a requirement for some housing – to be designed by Smith, and the work subjected to his approval. One of the earliest sites to be developed under Smith's guidance was Dog Kennel Field. The developer was Coles Child. Coal was his basic trade.

COLES CHILD

William Coles Child's family business, of coal, iron, cement and lime, was based on the Lambeth river-side, at Belvedere Wharf, near today's South Bank Centre. The business was typical of many that were beginning to take advantage of the expansion in canals, railways, and industry generally. Coles Child was only in his late teens when he took on the family business after his father's death. Five years later he approached Morden College for the tenancy of a portion of the 'Great Meadow', which stretched, between The Thames, the Enderby works and what is now Pelton Road. He wanted to '*form wharves, and erect manufactories thereon*'.

Morden College told Child that in return for a lease at East Greenwich he would be expected to spend at

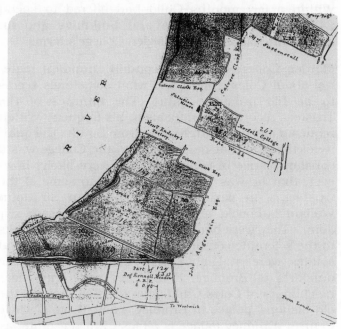

Plan produced by Morden College showing area covered by Coles Child's estate. Reproduced by kind pemission of the Trustees of the Martin Collection.

least £3,000 on 'substantial buildings, a road, an embankment,and drainage' - making it quite clear that what was expected was an 'advantageous development'. As negotiations proceeded they intimated that they also expected housing to be built there. Within a few months Child had offered to spend £4,000 on embankments and buildings and an agreement was made on Morden College's terms.

Morden College's archives contain abundant material about Coles Child's and what sometimes seems to be his nuisance value. The Minutes of the Trustees record their refusals to his frequent written requests together with reports from Smith. The quality of the coal that he supplied to the College was a constant cause of complaint. It is very likely, however, that he was personally known to some of the trustees - in particular the Chairman Sir John William Lubbock, and his son and successor, Sir John. They were bankers with strong personal links to the scientific community. The Lubbock home and estates were at High Elms, Farnborough, on the outskirts of Bromley, Kent. They were thus near neighbours of Coles Child who, in 1846, bought the old bishops' palace in Bromley – now Bromley Civic Centre. Bromley Palace is almost, but not quite, as grand as it sounds. Child's life style would have been eclipsed by the Lubbocks at High Elms. J.L. Filmer, who wrote about Child's life in Bromley, speculated that some of his wealth came from selling his Belvedere Road wharf to the Charing Cross Railway in 1863. He was involved with many railway companies in Kent and sat on their boards while deriving profits from commodity sales to them.

Railways are great consumers of coal and coke and

a good investment for someone whose money came from the haulage of bricks and coal. Coles Child seems to have set himself to transform the market town of Bromley by his intervention in public affairs and his specially grown prize winning hops. He also intervened in Greenwich politics - as described in a later chapter. His grave is the most prominent in Bromley churchyard.

COAL

Industrial development on the Greenwich riverside quickly went ahead, The river wall was rebuilt and by 1840 Coles Child had erected limekilns and coke ovens. Gravel from Morden College sites at Blackheath Point was used for these projects. He also considered building a tramway along the Willow Dyke - already taking shape as Pelton Road.

In the 1840s haulage companies, which today use lorries, were based on sailing barges and they diversified into making the bricks and lime that they carried routinely for others. It is still easy to see the scars of the chalk pits down river at Northfleet and Grays and around the Medway. Many cement manufacturers began their profession as lime burners. Coal was brought from north east ports by fleets of colliers which often carried a cargo of lime on their return trip. It is this trade which Coles Child served. In the eighteenth century lime burning had been an important industry in the Greenwich area, often on sites owned by Morden College to the east of Greenwich South Street and Lewisham Road. Many of these sites were used for residential development in the late eighteenth and early nineteenth century. Pits from which chalk and ballast were dug could be found between Greenwich and Woolwich and at the back of what is now Maze Hill Station and at Charlton Football Ground.

In 1840 Child was 'pleased to announce' his facilities in the *Kentish Mercury*. Coals and coke could be supplied *'at a considerable reduction in price because of the facilities possessed by no other house'* for *'purchase of coals at the pit's mouth'*. In Greenwich coal could be *'loaded directly from the hold of the ship into the wagons'* thus *'avoiding contingencies caused by severe weather and half the usual breakage'*. He boasted that they were the *'largest manufacturers of oven coke'* and that orders to *'railways, maltsters, ironfounders and consumers'* would be *'executed with probity, punctuality and dispatch'*.[22]

Child's activities, aided by Morden College and George Smith, made a visual impact on East Greenwich which continues, - mainly because he built so much housing of a reasonable standard. The wharves, which he developed, are still there and still in use.

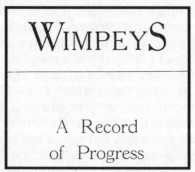

Frontispiece to a Wimpey publicity brochure of 1926.

MOWLEM

Coles Child intended to lease riverside sites to commercial interests but initially there were problems. In 1841 a limeburner Mr. Walker was on and off site in a year and eventually failed because Coles Child had to take over the works and offer *'Grey stone and other limes on as advantageous terms as any house in the trade'.*[23] A soap-works also had a brief appearance and closed, following complaints about the smell. In 1852 the largest part of the riverside area, to be known in future as Granite Wharf, was leased to Mowlem, Burt and Freeman – for a while it was a depot for Wimpey and is now operated by Tarmac, but is essentially in the same ownership and use.

The most visible symbol of the stone trades carried out in Greenwich is at Swanage. The Great Globe at Durlston Head was made in Mowlem's Stone Yard at Greenwich and shows that this works once had more pretensions than the cartage of aggregate. John Mowlem came from Swanage and worked in the stone quarries there before coming to London. By the time his Greenwich works was opened he had built up a large and successful business. In retirement he returned to live in Swanage and then began to remodel the town and fill it with mementoes of his work in London. The Great Globe is 10 feet in diameter, and weighs 40 tons. It is made up of 15 segments of Portland Stone and its surface is carved in great detail with a map of the world. It was given to Swanage by Mowlem's successor, George Burt. Why was it made in Greenwich and then moved - presumably by sea? In Swanage it stands on the cliff top surrounded by a strange collection of relics of municipal street furniture culled from London streets.

It may be that there are relics of the Globe in Greenwich if anyone could identify them. Old photographs indicate that it was probably made alongside a rough wall - very similar to a wall of random stone that still runs between Cadet Place and the old Mowlem site's boundary. This wall contains stones of many shapes and types. Are any of these discarded pieces of the Globe?

At the end of Cadet Place the inlet was once called 'Dead Dog Bay' because of the carcasses of domestic pets washed up there – or, allegedly on some occasions, dead sheep.

Naz and Mary Wright admire the Swanage
Globe in 1947. Photograph Harry Wright.

HOUSES

Having got the riverside industrial sites in place Coles Child turned to housing development. In the early 1840s he took over the rest of Great Meadow from Morden College with the condition that he drained ponds and dykes. Some portions of land were set aside for use in brick making. The first houses were built in 1842 and building continued for the next twenty years.

Sub-leases to builders were vetted by Morden College, before being awarded by Child. George Smith, as College Surveyor, monitored the design of the houses and in some cases made proposals himself.

There were sanctions against Child if substandard or unsuitable housing was built - for instance in 1853 he was told that no further leases would be granted unless some lower grade properties were abandoned. He was sometimes reprimanded for not sticking closely enough to Smith's designs.

THE DURHAM COALFIELD

The street names of the area reflect Coles Child business interests. 'Pelton Road' is the main road through the estate and 'The Pelton Arms' on the corner was no doubt aimed at the thirsty crews of colliers and riverside workers. Pelton Main was a major colliery in the Durham coalfield - the source of the coal in which Coles Child dealt. Waldridge, the original name for Christchurch Way, is another colliery in the same area.

Although some street names have changed the original names were usually taken from the Durham coalfield.

Banning Street was originally 'Chester (le Street) Street, a town in Durham near Pelton and Waldridge. Derwent Street is probably a reference to the River Derwent, which flows near Chester le Street – or to the Derwent Ironworks nearby. Thornley, Whitworth and Caradoc are all names of coal mines, elsewhere in the Durham coalfield. Braddyll, was the name of a coal owner, after which a railway and - today - a preserved locomotive are named.

At one time terraces within these roads had separate names and these too had coalfield related names -'Lambton Terrace' in Pelton Road referred to a colliery in the Durham coalfield, as did Stanley Terrace.

Although much of this housing is now in private hands on several buildings can still be seen Morden College's distinctive 'Invicta' plaque - often mistaken for a fire insurance sign.

WHITEWAY

Coles Child continued to expand and gradually took on more parcels of land from Morden College for development. In due course he retired to his home in Bromley and William Whiteway, who had been his

Waldridge Colliery from W.T.Hair, Views of the Collieries, 1844

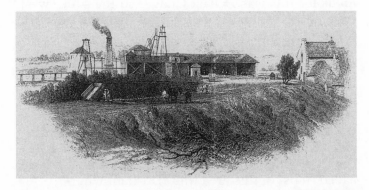

Pelton Colliery from W.T.Hair, Views of the Collieries, 1844

manager, took over the business in partnership with a Mr. Rowton. Whiteway was active in local politics and a keen conservative. He built 11 Westcombe Park Road and lived there.

COLLIERS AND THE COAL TRADE

In the nineteenth century coal ships from north east England, 'colliers', began to crowd out the River, as more coal came from the North Eastern ports to supply London's industry.

Adjacent to Greenwich marsh were areas very important to the organisation of the coal trade. In the 1830s, down river at Charlton, 'collier stands' were developed where ships waited their turn to go into the wharves where their cargoes of coal would be unloaded. The system to regulate the incoming traffic, based on the Coal Exchange in London, was reordered in the early 1840s and one of the key areas for this was Ballast Quay – on the south west edge of the Peninsula and part of the area in which Coles Child was active.

Railway companies developed their own coal delivery network around London based on collier ships coming into Poplar Dock on the opposite side of the River. Colliers had to wait in Bugsby's Reach to enter the Dock at Blackwall. Slightly down river of Angerstein Wharf in Charlton, William Cory erected a vast coal handling plant mounted on a floating platform called *Atlas*. In this area was 'Durham Wharf'.

No one should underestimate the importance of this

coal trade to London - without it the capital city would have remained medieval. Coal provided the power and raw materials that allowed the city to grow.

It was with great excitement in 1852 that the *John Bowes* was received in Poplar Dock loaded with coal from the north east of England. She was the first purpose built steam collier to carry coal to London and she opened up a whole new era of coal delivery. Steam driven carriers could carry more coal with more reliability down the treacherous East Coast than could the sailing ships.

After 1870 the use of 'sea coal' from the Tyne ports escalated and it appealed to new customers who needed a regular large supply of coal. Large gas works and power stations were built on both sides of the River in east and south east London because this coal supply was available.

Design for elevations on the Coles Child Estate. Reproduced by kind permission Trustees of the Martin Collection.

Colliers at the East Greenwich Gas Works jetty. From A Century of Gas in South London.

7. DEVELOPERS

George Smith continued to manage Morden College and the Mercers Company's holdings on the Marsh. His energy and initiative transformed Greenwich Marsh, and much else in Greenwich beside. Site after site was parcelled up, a developer found, and the site leased with clear instructions for good quality buildings and respectable sub-tenants.

It is also remarkable that most of these chosen leaseholders were making an investment themselves in industries dependent on coal tar – a waste product of the new gas industry. Gas industry waste products in the period are usually thought of as a nuisance – polluting, dangerous and an expensive problem. However coal tar was being bought, processed and used as a raw material by people who had every expectation of making a lot money.

This is not just another example of a coal-based economy at work - these industrialists needed the processing ability of the gas industry. With some irony it might be said that the Greenwich Peninsula was made what it is on the one hand by George Smith and Morden College and on the other hand by the gas industry.

BRYAN AND HOWDEN

John Bryan and Gidley Howden were almost the earliest developers identified by Morden College. They had a works on Bankside and wanted to expand. They made coal gas manufacturing apparatus - one of many companies in the iron trade who were then taking advantage of the rapidly expanding gas industry. A third partner in the business, who probably provided the finance, was a Charles Holcombe.

John Bryan had been responsible for the building and setting up of a number of gas works throughout southern England – with varying degrees of financial success and subsequent recriminations from local people. In this he was typical of several operators in this trade.

In 1837 Bryan and Howden took a ninety nine year lease on a plot, previously used to grow osier, to the north of Great Pitts. Anything they built needed to be approved by George Smith. Problems soon began to arise.

In 1839 Morden College discovered that they were unable to obtain insurance on the site because of the 'extremely hazardous business' being carried out there. This was tar distilling and it was reported that the premises 'consists of three brick buildings - one a cooperage, another for the boiler and rectifying plant, and another for the tar still'.[24] By this time coal tar from the gas industry was available at knock down prices and the flourishing shipbuilding industries of the lower Thames provided a ready market for weather proofing products. Throughout the area many entrepreneurs were experimenting with cheap coal tar in the hope of making a saleable product from it.

Complaints began to made about the nature of Bryan and Howden's work from several quarters and it appeared that *'oily matter was running about'.*[24] The partnership was in financial trouble and Charles Holcombe wrote to Morden College to say that he no longer had any connection with the partnership.

In 1841 Morden College offered the site to other potential tenants. One offer came from Holcombe himself and another from an Arthur Hills of Battersea. He was the brother of Frank Hills and, as we shall see, the Hills family was to make their fortunes from gas industry waste products – as Bryan and Howden had tried to do and failed. The first tenant had been a failure, others were to do rather better.

JOHN BETHELL

It is not clear exactly when John Bethell first moved to his site on the west bank of the Marsh. The earliest correspondence in the Morden College archive dates from 1839 when he made an offer for 20 acres of land and was turned down. Two months later he was negotiating with them on buildings to be erected and the route of a road. His tenancy with them must be almost the longest on the Marsh, since his successor company, The Improved Wood Paving Co., lasted well into the twentieth century – they are still shown on maps in the 1930s. Bethell's work on the development of coal tar as a preservative will be taken up again.

CHARLES HOLCOMBE

In 1841 Morden College granted a lease on a large site - 'Further Pitts' - to Charles Holcombe who by then had taken over some of the land previously leased to Bryan and Howden. Like Coles Child, Holcombe acted as a developer, leasing part of the site to a network of other companies.

Holcombe was a rich man - only three years earlier he had taken occupation of Valentines Park, a large mansion in Ilford. His family were local benefactors in the Ilford area. A younger generation were named 'Ingleby'. A road alongside Valentine's House is named after him 'Holcombe Road'. Strangely, the adjacent road is 'Bethell Avenue' - and this is unlikely to be a coincidence – did Holcombe have some sort of partnership with Bethell? That these two Greenwich developers of coal tar products are remembered in Ilford road names must have some undiscovered significance.

In Greenwich directories Holcombe's works on the marsh is given as a '*brass foundry, tar and Asfelt works*'. He is also described as a '*refiner of coal tar, spirit, pitch and varnish*'. So, like many others in the 1840s, he was experimenting with gas industry tars for use in paint and varnish.

Holcombe built Morden Wharf. It is not known why he called it this - perhaps he had a special relationship with Morden College, or wanted to curry favour with them. He built a road, known as Morden Lane or Morden Wharf Road which still runs through the Amylum Works although it no longer gives access to the River.

Like Coles Child, Holcombe wanted to improve the property which he had leased and gave this as his reason when he asked Morden College for permission to lay asphalt on the river path. He also asked permission to build a draw dock and complained when permission had been given to someone else to deposit rubbish on the riverside. He built houses, inevitably designed by George Smith of Morden College.

These activities gradually added to the local amenities and made the area more attractive to other incoming industrialists.

THE SEA WITCH

On the riverbank Holcombe built a public house called the Sea Witch. The site of the pub is now covered by Amylum's riverside laboratory block – a building that seems to look very much like its predecessor. The pub had a riverside garden separated from it by the roadway.

In a photograph of the 1930s the brewery is shown as Whitbread, but earlier it had been Gurney Hanbury of Camberwell.

'Sea Witch' was probably named after a ship - it was a common name but it might be speculated that it was named after the American tea clipper of revolutionary design which was soon to visit the Thames. The pub was destroyed in 1940.

WILLIS AND WRIGHT

Another partnership which acted as developers was Willis and Wright, the owners of Champion's Vinegar Brewery on the corner of Old Street and City Road in Shoreditch. Elizabeth Champion was a signatory to the lease. In the 1840s they were allocated the area of Greenwich Marsh known as 'Horseshoe Breach'.

By 1845 Willis and Wright had built '*a tar factory, house, chemical factory, and buildings*'. It caused some nuisance and complaints were made about leakage of '*noxious matter*' from the plant. It is not clear why vinegar makers should open a tar distillery but in 1846 they advertised that they made '*vinegar, mustard, acetic acid and naphtha*'.[25] Naphtha is oil distilled from coal tar. Willis and Wright eventually signed a lease with Morden College in 1850. This was with the usual expectation on Morden College's part that they would undertake development work at Horseshoe Breach. The site was inspected by George Smith and discussions on the work began. A year went by and nothing happened. Further discussion ensued about a wharf and buildings but complaints continued. Ten years later Morden College complained that nothing had been done.

Willis and Wright left Greenwich in the early 1860s having let some sub tenancies. Horseshoe Breach had an interesting future in other hands.

8. AN ENGINEERING INTERLUDE

Engineering was a dominant trade in 'Kentish London' with several important companies in the Deptford and Creekside area. Penn's works is particularly well known, but they were not the only ones. Very few engineering works were located on the Marsh - rather they clustered round the older industrial area on Deptford Creek. The exceptions were established businesses looking for a 'greenfield' site. Of these, the earliest and most interesting was Joshua Beale.

A MOVE FROM WAPPING

Joshua Taylor Beale was a Wapping cabinetmaker who had prospered with a design for a rotary steam engine. His next invention was a safe method of heating inflammable liquids - important to local manufacturers of both sugar and tar. He developed a lamp, which used some of the new fuels made from gas industry by-products, which were becoming available. In the early 1830s Beale needed to expand when he moved into a purpose built factory on Greenwich Marsh as a tenant of the Enderbys.

STEAM ROAD VEHICLES

One of Beale's projects in Greenwich was a steam driven road vehicle. He worked with a Colonel Maceroni who was a Sicilian born but brought up in Manchester. It was said that - '*he retained a love of quick motion*' [26]- hence his interest in steam road vehicles.

One of Maceroni's other interests was in the use of coal tar for road surfaces. He said that the first-ever tarred garden path was laid in Blackheath in the garden of a Mr. Bell' - is 'Bell' perhaps a misprint for 'Beale' and is this how the two got to know each other?

In 1841 Maceroni set up the 'Common Road Steam Conveyance Company' to make steam cars. He asked Joshua Beale and his brother Benjamin to make them for him since his own factory in Paddington was besieged by bailiffs. To get publicity for their cars Beale and Maceroni began to go on trips round the district. In July 1840 Maceroni took a party of seventeen from Greenwich to Lewisham and then to Bromley. On the way back they turned onto the Dover Road and went up Blackheath Hill - at 12 miles per hour '*in gallant style*'.[27] They continued up Shooters Hill and stopped at The Bull to fill the boiler. Inevitably, water was not all they took on, and - *'the men were regaled and eulogised the scientific engineer'*. [28]

Maceroni had agreed to pay Beale £800 for each carriage but because Benjamin Beale had changed the design in order to make it work he was charged an extra £300. This money was not forthcoming and so Beale impounded the carriages. No more was heard of them and this pioneering attempt to make steam driven vehicles, which would run on ordinary roads, came to an end.

Beale and Macaroni were not alone. At around the same time Frank Hills was also building steam cars in Greenwich. He had a chemical works in Deptford and by the mid-1840s had moved onto the East Greenwich Tide Mill site - his work there as an industrial chemist is described below. In the 1840s he was rivalling Beale with trips up Shooters Hill and beyond, with two different prototype steam driven vehicles.

Mr. Hills Steam Road Carriage. From Mechanics' Magazine'.

THE EXHAUSTER

Many other things were made at Beale's riverside works in Greenwich - a propeller and a way of preventing 'encrusting' in boilers by using urine and soda. Beale was also involved in the design of equipment for the early gas industry. He tried to make gas cookers - at a time when such an idea was revolutionary - but accusations of spying from other manufacturers put an end to his work.

Beale's most successful idea was for the 'exhauster' - a pump in reverse used to draw gas from retorts in gas works. His exhauster patents were sold to Bryan Donkin, whose engineering works were in Bermondsey. They moved to Chesterfield where they developed Beale's ideas.

Beale's Exhauster.

Joshua Beale lived very near his works. His home, called 'Conduit House was on the corner of Vanbrugh Hill and Trafalgar Road - where the Granada Cinema was later built. His son John moved nearer Blackheath and built 'Heathview' in Westcombe Park Road in 1883. John continued his father's work. He designed a sort of magic lantern - one of a number of forerunners of 'moving pictures' - called a 'choeutoscope'. It was similar to a machine known as the 'Wheel of Life' or 'Zoetrope' in which little figures cut on a drum appeared to move when revolved at high speed.

PENNY FARTHINGS

'Penny farthing' bicycles were originally known as 'ordinaries'. John Beale invented a version of the 'ordinary' which he called 'The Facile' advertised as '*suitable for the young and athletic and the elderly*' - although, unless the rider was careful he or she could '*come a cropper*'. At Heathview there is a large circular flowerbed which is supposed to be where John Beale's bicycle test track ran. The testing was done by his teenage sons who toured Kent with one of the many cycling clubs for young men of the period.

Sadly many of John Beale's inventions were not made in Greenwich but by specialist manufacturers under licence. The Greenwich works was closed to become part of the Telcon cable works. Beale's factory had been of a type common in London - that of the resourceful general engineer constantly designing and making new devices and who could turn his hand to almost anything.

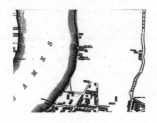

9. BRITISH CARBOLIC

The manufacture of soap is an important part of the chemical industry and of significance in nineteenth century London. The Thames Soap Works, on the site of what is now the Amylum refinery, was owned by a company called Wilkie and Soames.

In the early nineteenth century London soap makers were taking advantage of new manufacturing processes and ideas as well as using abundant supplies of raw materials from south seas whaling and the products of colonial exploitation, like coconuts. All of the biggest and most profitable soap works were in London and they flourished along with the closely related candle making industry.

THE SOAMESES

The Soames family had had a soap works in Wheeler Street, Spitalfields, since 1809 but their original partner, Mr Wilkie, had died in 1821. Their' Spital-

Soames heading by kind permission Morden College

fields works was the tenth largest soap works in the country but the need to expand - and maybe the construction of Commercial Street - persuaded them to move to Greenwich.

> WILKIE & SOAMES'
> CELEBRATED
> COLD WATER SOAP.

The Soames family had lived in Greenwich and Blackheath for many years. James Soames had moved to the Red House in Maze Hill in 1849 while his son, another James, was in charge of the soap works. His brother, Henry Aldwin Soames, who also lived locally was a 'Russia merchant' – probably an importer of Russian tallow, another raw ingredient of soap.

The Soames family were dominant in Greenwich church life. William Aldwin Soames was Vicar of Greenwich and James Soames, Jnr., paid for the building of a new church in the expanding East Greenwich suburbs. This was St. George's Church in Kirkside Road, Westcombe Park, and the living went to another brother, Henry Kolle Soames.

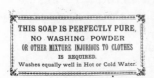

> THIS SOAP IS PERFECTLY PURE,
> NO WASHING POWDER
> OR OTHER MIXTURE INJURIOUS TO CLOTHES
> IS REQUIRED.
> Washes equally well in Hot or Cold Water.

Several Soameses were active in Greenwich politics. James Soames held local office, and his son, Walter, was Mayor of Greenwich before the First World War. They took part in local electioneering – and as late as the 1920s the company made an advertising film hoping to influence the General Election. Walter's daughter, Olave, was to become internationally known by marrying Baden-Powell, and becoming Chief Guide.

Morden College Trustees were clearly impressed when James Soames approached them for an under-lease on part of the Holcombe site. They had already had numerous dealings with the Rev. William Aldwin Soames on various local charitable causes, including the construction of Christ Church, East Greenwich and expected high standards of such an important local family. When bricks for building the soapworks were made on site the College waived the usual royalties.

MADE ONLY BY
WILKIE & SOAMES,
GREENWICH.
BEWARE OF
WORTHLESS IMITATIONS.

THE THAMES STEAM SOAP WORKS

The Thames Steam Soap Works - later Thames Soap and Candle Factory - was highly profitable. It employed more than 140 men and boys and James Soames boasted that he con-tributed to good works in the neighbourhood from the money he made. In 1864 the works had spe-cial departments for glycerine and paraffin as well as soap boiling and candle making. There was a laboratory, stables and maintenance department, separate toilets and canteens for men and women workers and housing for the gatekeeper and house-keeper

The company's slogan was 'Greenwich the world standard in both soap and time'. The soaps included 'Apron',

WILL DO MORE WORK
IN THE WASH TUB WITH
LESS LABOUR THAN ANY OTHER SOAP.
THE PERFECTION OF SOAP.

'Big Wilkie', 'Spry', 'Wonderful Washer' and 'British Carbolic'[29] - no-nonsense, heavy-duty cleansers for the hardworking housewife in her war against dirt and disease. They also made candles - Greenwich Sperm and Stearaffine.

Towards the end of the nineteenth century Wilkie and Soames ceased to be an independent business. New, giant soap companies from the north of England threatened the older London industry. Wilkie and Soames fought off take-over bids from 1902 onwards but were eventually swallowed up by Unilever who closed the Greenwich factory in the 1930s. Some traces of the soap works remain inside the Amylum factory where a couple of old walls - much shored up - still advertise Thames Soap Works. The Soames family represented a type of industrialist that was not usual in Greenwich. Most local factory owners were content to let local events take their course – to use the workforce and its skills, and move on. Soames lived and worked in the community and tried to get it into their way of thinking – Church of England and Liberal although, to quote Neil Rhind, 'James Soames gift of a church to the community was to some extent inspired by nepotism'.[30] This style of philanthropy was to be made famous by another soap manufacturer, William Lever at Port Sunlight. Lever was to quarrel about treatment of the workforce with George Livesey, whose co-partnership scheme at the East Greenwich Gas Works is described in a later chapter.

10. BRICKS AND MORTAR

All the activity in building factories, workshops and housing used a lot of bricks and cement. After 1840 cement manufacture was to play a big part in the Peninsula's industry. Before that there had been some brick making with several patches of brick earth under exploitation.

THOMAS TAYLOR

Thomas Taylor was the earliest recorded brickmaker on Greenwich marsh. He had been George Russell's foreman at the brickworks on the site which preceded the Tide Mill at the end of Marsh Lane (Riverway). It was Taylor who had incited his colleague, Mr. Bignall, to throw, Philip Sharpe, the Wall Reeve, into the river in 1796.

Thomas Taylor is listed as a landowner 'on the Level' from about 1800 – probably meaning 'land in Pear Tree Marsh'. Six years later he was a sub-tenant of George Moore, apparently at Horseshoe Breach. The investment was made jointly with Thomas Tickner, landlord of the Noah's Ark pub, Deptford, and they were still there in 1818. Taylor is said to be living at 'Bank Place, Greenwich', and this could be an unidentified building which preceded East Lodge.

JABEZ HOLLICK

The earliest and perhaps the longest lasting cement works came to Greenwich in 1841.

Cement manufacture had been all round Greenwich, but not actually in it, for several years. Manufacture was concentrated along the Thames and Medway and developments in the early years of the nineteenth century had transformed it into one of the leading industrial sectors. There was a wide variety of different types of artificial stone and concrete and as many manufacturers as there were patents and ideas. Most works – certainly the most famous - were down river around Swanscombe and Greenhithe although there were some cement and stone factories on the Isle of Dogs before 1840.

Hollick leased a site at Greenwich from Holcombe in 1849. He seems to have had an earlier short lived works on part of the old Enderby site and also a works at Borstal in the Medway valley (another important area for cement manufacture). In 1849 Hollick gave his address as Warwick Cottages which then stood at the Marsh Lane end of Morden Wharf Road. He later moved somewhere grander, initially Maze Hill, and then 132 Coleraine Road.

His cement works, adjacent to Morden Wharf, had a

long river frontage with a loading dock. There was a sailmakers shop, a 'bone' store and a 'snowcrete house'- perhaps a storehouse or a demonstration building. The works was eventually taken over by the Associated Portland Cement Manufacturers before the First World War but it was still in operation by them in 1935 and the area is still sometimes known as Hollick's Wharf in the 1990s.

Since the industry was mainly concentrated down river, what was the advantage to Hollick of coming so far upstream? Did he want to be nearer to the centres of intensive building operations? Most of the downstream works used chalk supplies from nearby pits, the vast scars of which are still a major feature of the Thameside landscape. Where did Hollick's raw materials come from?

GEORGE CROWLEY ASHBY

The East Greenwich Portland Cement Works was set up by George Crowley Ashby. The Ashby family were Quakers, based in Staines. George's father, William had been involved in the family bank and had had a barge haulage business dealing in building materials. He also made Roman Cement in Staines.

Why did the Ashbys came to Greenwich to make cement? It may be relevant that George's middle name was 'Crowley' – implying a link with the Quaker ironfounders who had, for a while, been based in Greenwich.

George Crowley Ashby took over the Staines business 1850 and moved to Greenwich leasing a site from Holcombe. It was at the back of Morden Wharf but had no river access. The works comprised a chalk mill, five chalk tanks (one very large) and two sets of coke ovens.

George Ashby died in 1893 and is buried in the Friends' Burial Ground in Staines. Like Hollick, Ashby's cement works was long lasting and was also taken over by APCM.

EVEN MORE CEMENT WORKS

There were several other cement works in Greenwich, all smaller and more short lived than Hollick's and Ashby's. One was owned by a John Winkfield and was situated apparently on the northern part of Enderby Wharf. It was probably taken over by Hollick. Later, between 1879-1894, a phosphate manufacturer called John Winkfield lived in St.John's Park, Blackheath, and it might be speculated that this was the same man. If so, as a Justice and Deputy Lieutenant of Kent, he was clearly someone with a political career.

A Henry Reid also had a cement works on part of Holcombe's holding where there were kilns, a dwelling house, a garden, a boiler and engine house. It seems to have lasted less than ten years.

Nearby William Angerstein, the local landowner, had a short-lived cement works for a while at the same period.

COMPOSITION

Close to cement is the manufacture of 'Composition' - this is a vague term and can mean a number of things like '*a new paving composition - .. pebbles in pitch*' or '*composition for sheathing, preserving etc. ships bottoms*'. The related "*Compo*" can mean anything from an unreliable mortar to a rubbery constituent of cricket balls. An 1826 recipe described a mixture of oil of turpentine and coal tar mixed with resin, size and ochre. More likely what was being made on the Greenwich Peninsula in the 1850s was something like James Wyatt's 1790s invention, "*compo-cement*", designed to be used for stucco.

SIR JOHN SCOTT LILLIE

Sir John Scott Lillie held a number of patents, including one, taken out in 1851, for road coverings. Others were for various devices in motive power and '*elastic fluids for the working of machinery*'. No doubt his Greenwich '*composition works*' made something to do with road making materials - probably a sort of concrete in the form of paving slabs.

WILLIAM BUCKWELL

William Buckwell's factory was yet another cement-type works on the northern part of the Enderby site. It was a '*composition works*' but it appears on some 1860s maps as '*old concrete works*'. Buckwell held a number of patents, taken out during the 1840s, for making pipes '*artificially in moulds*' and '*compressing fuel*' which implies the manufacture of briquettes (usually a mixture of coal dust and tar). He also held patents for both scaffolding and steam engines.

There are scant details about Buckwell's Greenwich works but rather more about his departure from the business world. He is said to have been a railway contractor as well as a manufacturer of artificial stone. Neither occupation can have been much of a success because in 1862 he disappeared. This was because he owed £90,000 - £50,000 of it to Italian creditors. He had been involved in the construction of a railway between Novara and Lake Orta – north west of Milan.

When Buckwell failed to turn up at a bankruptcy hearing in London, Mr. Haydon, of the City Detectives, went to Turin to look for him. He was found at Borgomanero, on the line of his railway, *'concealed between the ceiling and roof of an outbuilding'*. Haydon wanted to take him back to London, but, of course, his Italian creditors wanted him to stay in Italy. The Italian authorities took him to the frontier with France at the top of Mount Cenis - but Haydon was tipped off and got there first. The Italian police escort refused to hand Buckwell over to Haydon but while they were talking to him, they inadvertently crossed the frontier by a few feet (it was high in the Alps and everyone was knee deep in snow). Because he was then in France. Buckwell was arrested by French police who said they would shoot him if he tried to escape back to Italy. Meanwhile the Italian soldiers refused to leave unless they could take him back to Turin. It was a very long and very cold night and the discussions were protracted but eventually Buckwell returned to London and gaol.

PATENT STONE AND HENRY BESSEMER

In 1866 Frederick Ransome came from Ipswich to take over a site roughly on the area of today's Victoria Wharf for a *'patent stone works'*. He described this as an *'immense factory...on an ugly and pestiferous marsh'.*[31] It is perhaps noteworthy that the site was partly owned by Henry Bessemer, the steel magnate.

By 1868 Ransome was in business with a counting house, chimney, wharf, jetty and so on. The stone making process was somewhat complicated but in essence the idea was to *'dissolve common flint'* and turn it into *'glue'*. This was used to bind pure sandstone with cement of silicate of lime. The result could be worked in a plastic state and later with a chisel like natural stone. It was said to produce *'carvings like the best Portland stone'.*[31]

The factory manager was Ernest Leslie Ransome who lived in Royal Hill Place with his wife, Mary, and two children. One of the agricultural implement making family, he had been Ipswich since 1844 and become interested in making artificial stoneware. This was an important Suffolk industry and a number of leading manufacturers came from there. Several of the Greenwich factory workers had come from Suffolk with Ransome and some lived near the works - including the publican of the Star in the East who came from Walton-on-the-Naze and whose brother in law, William Brooks from Mistley, was an architectural draughtsman in the stone works.

Plaque embedded in the platform of Chester Station.
Picture kind permission Tim Smith.

John Felgate the gatekeeper came from Suffolk.
Some of the stonework made in the Greenwich
factory still survives. Anyone who travels to Chester
Station will find the company's identification plaque
embedded in the ground in front of the Exit Stair-
case. In Greenwich some of the company's name-
plates can be seen in the pavement of St.John's
Park. It is probable that a great deal more remains
to be discovered.

The Ransome factory was only short-lived. By 1878
it had been taken over by Hodges and Butler. Ernest
Leslie Ransome went to America in 1872 where he
founded the Ransome Concrete Co. - famous for wire
rope in a cable car system which withstood the 1906
earthquake. Frederick Ransome himself died in Dul-
wich, 20 years later.

HODGES, BUTLER AND DALE

Hodges, Butler and Dale, took over the stone works from Ransome and it is intriguing that after this date the rates were paid in the name of Henry Bessemer, himself as owner. In the future the factory was variously known as 'Thames Silicated Stone' or 'Imperial Stone' and the area became known as 'Imperial Wharf'.

The company was owned by a James William Butler who lived in Montpelier Vale, Blackheath and John Anderson, a cement manufacturer from Faversham, who was also involved in a works at Upnor.

PAVING SLABS

A number of works were opened after the Second World War, which specialised in the manufacture of paving slabs. These included The London Phosphate Syndicate, concrete slab manufacturer, W. Rees, concrete slab manufacturer and the Rheocrete Paving Stone Slab Co.

11. HARD STEEL & BIG GUNS

Something seems to have been going on in the 1860s - industries on the Greenwich Peninsula took off with astonishing speed. Suddenly some big names started to arrive. There was initially an emphasis on shipbuilding but then steel works and big guns moved in. In so far as Henry Bessemer and A.T.Blakeley are concerned it seems likely that there was a sub text, which has never been, and may never be, explained. With these industries, as with some others of the same era, the stakes were high and the backers came from the world of international banking. The decline in this rise to the industrial main stage was probably caused by the Overend Gurney banking crash of 1866.

Some very important companies moved to the west bank of the Peninsula during this time. Some of them seem to have been unduly secretive. It is clear that there was some liaison between at least two of them.

HENRY BESSEMER

Perhaps the most famous industrialist to have taken a site at Greenwich was the steel magnate, Henry Bessemer. Steel production, together with Bessemer and his 'converter' , are usually associated with the north of England, and Sheffield in particular. It may come as a surprise to learn that Bessemer himself lived in South London and built a steel works at Greenwich. It has proved very difficult to find out anything very much about this works and there is some conflict of evidence about what really went on there – so much so as to raise a question – what was Bessemer really doing at East Greenwich?

Henry Bessemer came from a French background and was an ingenious inventor who held numerous patents on all sorts of devices and processes from which he made a lot of money. One of the earliest was 'bronze powder', which he made in a factory near St. Pancras. He described some of the lengths he went to in order to keep the process secret and, similarly, his, unfinished, autobiography is often very difficult to disentangle. Historians have suggested that his steel making process arose from his interest in making guns, something that, of course, would draw him to Woolwich and the Arsenal. Bessemer had been in France working with the French military authorities when he came to the conclusion that a new sort of metal was needed. In due course he developed a process and opened a works in Sheffield in the late 1850s. To cut a very long story very short indeed - he became involved with Col. Eardley Willmot at the Royal Arsenal and plans were made to build a plant for the manufac-

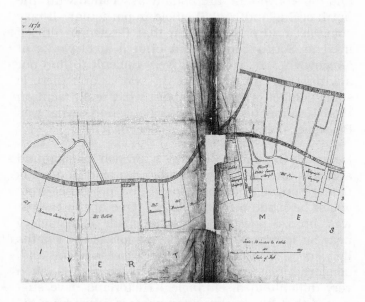

Plan. c.1871 showing Bessemer's site alongside others in the area. Reproduced kind permission London Borough of Greenwich, Woodlands Local History Library.

ture of Bessemer's steel there. It soon became clear that this support was not shared by the Minister of War and Bessemer's steel was rejected for use in the Arsenal. Bessemer was very bitter *'it was quite clear that neither I, nor my steel, was wanted at Woolwich, and I made up my mind to leave the place severely alone in future.'* [32]

The position at Woolwich was further complicated by the appointment in 1859 of William Armstrong; the Newcastle based arms manufacturer, to the position of Director of Rifled Ordnance at Woolwich.

Bessemer's son added a final, posthumous, chapter to Bessemer's autobiography. In this chapter is the only mention of the steel works that was built at Greenwich in the mid-1860s. The works was on the site now known as Victoria Wharf - one of the few sites on the Greenwich riverside which is not owned by Morden College. In June 1865 'Bessemer Brothers' asked for permission from the Thames Conservators to build a jetty. Later that year an advertisement in the *Kentish Mercury* mentions the closeness of the Bessemer works and its thirsty steelworkers to the Star in the East pub. The works was very small and it was intended that it should be run by Bessemer's sons. Bessemer Jnr says, *"It had two 2½ ton converters and all the plant necessary. Including one 2½-ton steam hammer and another ... the buildings were carefully designed, with the intention that the establishment should be in all respects be a model one"*. He went on to explain that it was, never opened because of the *"down turn in Thames ship-building"*. [33]

ENGINEERING. [JAN. 5, 1866.

THE BLAKELY ORDNANCE COMPANY, LIMITED,

Are prepared to Manufacture GUNS of any required Description, Pattern, or Size, whether on Captain Blakely's or any other System.

ALL ORDERS TO BE SENT TO THE OFFICE, No. 11, PALL MALL EAST, LONDON, S.W.—J. R. HAMILTON, Secretary.

HENRY BESSEMER & Co.,

SHEFFIELD,

MANUFACTURERS (BY THE BESSEMER PROCESS) OF

CAST STEEL

MARINE CRANK and OTHER SHAFTS, ORDNANCE, LOCOMOTIVE DOUBLE CRANK and STRAIGHT AXLES, TYRES, PISTON RODS, SHAFTS, CRANK PINS, and USES GENERALLY.

SOFT CAST STEEL IN BARS AND RODS, FOR MACHINERY PURPOSES.

BEST CAST STEEL FOR TOOLS, &c.

CASTINGS IN STEEL TO PATTERN.

Blakeley and Bessemer advertisements share the same page in a copy of Engineering

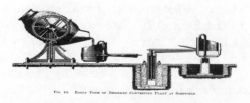

FIG. 44. EARLY FORM OF BESSEMER CONVERTING PLANT AT SHEFFIELD

An early form of Bessemer converter plant at Sheffield. From H. Bessemer, 'An Autobiography.'

WHAT HAPPENED TO THE GREENWICH STEEL WORKS?

The eventual fate of the Greenwich steel works is not clear. Bessemer Jnr. said that both works and plant were let to the London Steel and Ordnance Co. – but whoever was behind that body is not known.

'Henry Bessemer' continues to be listed in the official records. In 1872 there was a complaint from Morden College that the *'Bessemer Steel Co.'* had encroached on their land. Mysteriously, in 1874, *'Bessemer's liquidators'* appear in the ratebooks. At the same time discussions had begun for Bessemer to lease 'a small field in the marshes' from Morden College for 21 years and they were delighted to learn that he was offering more than the market value for it – not the action of someone who does not want a site. As late as 1891 Morden College's surveyor was still dealing with 'Bessemer Brothers'.

From about 1878 all or part of the works was let to Appleby Brothers and almost twenty years later, the site was let to a linoleum manufacturer, who later bought the freehold. The really interesting thing is what the linoleum manufacturer had to say about the site. His name was Frederick Walton and perhaps he knew Henry Bessemer – another of Bessemer's interests was linoleum. He certainly had a lot in common with him. Walton said how pleased he was to get the site because it was *'where Bessemer proved his widely known steel process'.*[34] Did Walton know something about the site that Bessemer wanted kept quiet? It is probably idle to speculate on what Bessemer was doing at Greenwich. Why did he omit to say anything about it himself?

Bessemer had moved to South London – to a very, very grand mansion indeed on Denmark Hill – in the early 1860s and a direct train service from Denmark Hill to Greenwich was planned. Perhaps he also thought that a steel works near his home would be useful. It would be tucked away from the prying eyes of his licensees at works in the north of England.

ALEXANDER THEOPHILUS BLAKELEY

There is something else, however, which concerns Bessemer's relationship with Greenwich and the manufacture of heavy ordnance. When Bessemer was first considering gun manufacture he had sought out the holder of a particularly important patent. This was Alexander Theophilus Blakeley, who had been described as 'the most significant British gun designer yet'.[35]

Blakeley however, like Bessemer, had been rejected by the military establishment and Woolwich Arsenal. No doubt both of them had good cause to feel aggrieved. In Britain most people with an interest in technology and warfare will have heard of William Armstrong and visited his beautiful Northumberland home, Cragside, near Rothbury. In 1859, William Armstrong was appointed as 'Superintendent of the Royal Gun Foundry for Rifled Ordnance' combining this with his work as owner of a large ordnance

The Blakeley gun manufactured for the Russian Government. From 'Illustrated London News'.

manufacturing concern at the Elswick Works in Newcastle. Only arms enthusiasts will have heard of Blakeley.

BLAKELEY GUNS ON SHOW

Blakeley is well known in America where some of his guns are exhibited. For example, in Grant Park, Galena, Illinois a cannon stands on display as ' *the Galena Blakeley*' and projectiles fired from it are shown at the US Military Academy. This gun, they will tell you, fired the opening salvo of the American Civil War at Fort Sumter in 1861 - it was '*the piece that really worried the beleaguered garrison. It was the sound of the future*'.[37] . It was a Blakeley gun which fired from the FSS Alabama – and this gun has recently been raised from the sunken ship and examined by the French Navy. In many American military museums Blakeley guns are exhibited and their role in the Civil War stressed.

Recently a Blakeley gun has been found in England, at Coalhouse Fort - downriver of Tilbury - and it is now displayed at Fort Nelson, Royal Armouries Museum, at Portsmouth, where an exhibition has been mounted about Blakeley's achievements. These guns, however, were all made in Liverpool because Blakeley did not have his own manufacturing base and guns were made for him at a variety of foundries. In 1863 he gave evidence to an Enquiry that 400 of his guns had already gone abroad. It appears that the British Government was not prepared to adopt Blakeley's system. His guns were

The Alabama, from Illustrated London News

required to meet what were said to be unrealistic standards in testing. There has been some comment of the role of William Armstrong in this. Armstrong was in the position of being both in charge of procuring and testing ordnance for the Government while being an arms manufacturer himself – something which would be seen today as a distinct conflict of interests. In 1859 Armstrong gave his patents to the nation and was knighted for his efforts. There has been more than a suggestion made that these patents incorporated elements of Blakeley's designs.

Blakeley was in touch with Morden College in 1863 and in 1864 signed an agreement with them. Although there is no indication in the Morden College records that any of the Trustees had taken an interest in Blakeley it might be noted that Thomas Baring, a trustee in the 1860s, had supported the Confederates - to whom Blakeley supplied guns - through Baring's Bank.

In 1865 Morden College gave Blakeley permission to build a Wharf on the site of what was later Ordnance Wharf. He discussed his proposals with the Metropolitan Board of Works - who sent their architect, Mr. Vuilliamy, down to inspect the site and Blakeley later applied to Quarter Sessions in order to put an official closure on a footpath alongside it.

However, Blakeley, and his still unfinished works, were in financial trouble and the Phoenix Gas Company noted that he was unable to pay for the gas supply they had laid on to the new works.

OPIUM DEALERS

Contemporary newspaper reports say that Blakeley was financed by a John Dent who sold his holdings in the company in 1865 and then went to China.

The deeds of the Blakeley site show that his backer was a Wilkinson Dent. Wilkinson Dent was the brother of Lancelot Dent - the man held ransom by the Chinese at the start of the first Opium War in 1841. Dent Brothers were opium traders - second only in size to Jardine Matheson, the bankers. For many years the Dent family were involved in the Chancery case on which Dickens may have based that in *Bleak House*. The collapse of the China House of Dent also led to the collapse of Blakeley - although he struggled to stay in business.

In September 1866 Blakeley wrote to Morden College giving his address as 11 Pall Mall East - just off Trafalgar Square, and a prosperous sounding location yet at the same time a petition of bankruptcy was being filed against him and a winding up order was announced in July. Meanwhile most of his Greenwich factory remained unused and unfinished. He died two years later in Peru.

It does not stretch the imagination too much to think that Henry Bessemer built his steel works to supply Blakeley with steel for guns and that the idea was to build an arms manufacturing complex at Greenwich

It is more than likely that by the time Bessemer died he no longer wanted to make public his keenness to sell big guns to foreign powers. Blakeley's downfall was due to a crisis of international finance - ultimately through Overend Gurney.

A codicil to this story is that Blakeley's half made guns remained on site for many years. South Metropolitan. Gas Co. used them as a feature on one of their gates and they were eventually sold for scrap in the 1970s - every one of them would now be a valuable collectors item.

SHANGHAE.—Advices are of the 6th instant.

OPIUM.—The large supplies of Malwa received from this port had caused a slight decline on previous quotations, but a brisk demand had led to considerable settlements at Tls. 577 a Tls. 580, at which latter price the market closed. Patna, after having been as low as Tls. 523, had rallied to Tls. 560, but closed rather weaker at Tls. 555.

	Malwa.	Bengal.
Estimated deliveries to 4th instant,	891 chests.	165 chests.
Estimated stocks on 4th instant,	1,892 ,,	205 ,,
With about 1,000 on the way up.		

EXCHANGE.—Business opened at 6/0¾ for Bank, and 6/1 a 6/1½ for Private Bills ; but closing rates advanced to 6/1 and 6/1½ a 6/2. Bank Drafts on Bombay, Rs. 296 ; on Hongkong, 10 days' sight, 24½ per cent. discount.
BULLION.—Mexican Dollars, Tls. 79.8.0 a Tls. 80 per $100. Pekin Gold, Tls. 163.5.0 a Tls. 164 per bar of Tls. 9.7.3.
FREIGHTS.—To London, Tea, £2.15 a £3 ; Cotton, £3.5. To New York, $15, nominal.

We annex a list of Arrivals and Departures,—and remain,

Dear Sir,

Yours faithfully,

DENT & Co.

Extract from Dent & Co.'s price list

12. SMALL GUNS AND AMMUNITION

While the manufacture of heavy armaments was ultimately unsuccessful in Greenwich, the manufacture of small-scale explosive devices continued there for many years.

THOMAS ROBSON

Thomas Robson had founded an ordnance works in Greenwich in 1845. This fronted onto the Woolwich Road with a path stretching back to a large area of land intersected by ditches and dykes. In this area were a number of huts in which work on the explosives was undertaken. In all probability some farming activities continued to be carried on – the only picture of Robson's works drawn in the 1880s shows a large and flourishing cabbage patch in front of one of the huts.

There were a number of other cartridge and small-scale explosive factories in the area from the 1870s. One of these was the Gladstone Cartridge Co. which

Scene of the explosion at the Cartridge Factory, Greenwich Marshes

shared the site with Henry Bessemer and the Ransome Stone Co. In the 1860s Billingsley and Munyard had a works - perhaps connected with Frederick Billingsley's ammunition works near the slaughterhouse

ROCKETS AND SIGNALS

Robson held patents for 'firing signals and other lights'.The factory turned out a variety of signalling devices for ships and railways, many of which were closely akin to fireworks. He also made 'proper' fireworks for displays and some other small scale explosive devices. After 1880 the works continued to carry Robson's name but was managed by James Dyer who lived with his wife and baby daughter in Wick Cottage (on the site of the fish and chip shop in Woolwich Road) adjacent to the works. Although the works covered a large area it employed relatively few people – eleven men, four women, and four boys.

A FATAL EXPLOSION

A great deal of the information which is available on the industries on the Greenwich Peninsula comes from accident reports. In the 1880s there were two accidents at Robson's. One item made was a railway fog signal, which consisted of two small iron saucers, enclosing a small amount of gunpowder. A large outer cup went over these with its edge 'crimped' to hold it closely together and the cups were then cemented and varnished. The 'crimping' was done by hand, using screw fly presses – an operation which carried 'some risk'. In fact there was at least one accidental explosion a month but owing to a 'misunderstanding' Mr. Dyer had not reported these accidents to the Explosives Inspectorate, as he was required to do by law.

Such operations were very carefully monitored and there was an iron shield, which moved between the worker and the explosives at the moment at which the pressing movement took place. There was also an arrangement to divert the flash outside the building should an explosion take place. Employees had to wear special shoes and fireproof clothes with no pockets in them.

20th November 1882 was Mary Mahoney's first day at work on the presses. Emily Gilder supervised her in one of the isolated huts. There was a space of six feet by five for the two women to sit with about 800 explosive signals. Unknown to Emily, Mary was putting the cups into the press in the wrong way. The foreman, Mr. Law, was standing about three yards outside the shed when he was knocked over by a series of explosions. He forced his way through the smoke to where Mary was lying on the floor among exploding powder, with molten lead falling on her. Despite his burns he managed to get her out and she said 'Oh, Mr.Law' as he tried to pull off her burning dress - until he too collapsed.

She was taken just across the road to the Workhouse Infirmary – now Greenwich District Hospital. 'Oh, Doctor, I was pressing of those fog signals when it went off ... I think I must have pressed it on the side'. She died four days later 'of exhaustion'.

Mary was twenty-four years old, and lived with her parents in Blackwall Lane. She was the eldest of four Greenwich family had taken in another young woman, Catherine Allman, as a lodger and she too worked at Dyer and Robson's.

On 11th June 1887 Catherine was at work making fireworks to be used as signals on the South Western Railway Steamers from Southampton. They were bright stars for 'Very Signal Cartridges', part of a large order for the Jubilee Naval Review.   The explosion, when it came, was *'like the firing of a pistol'*. It was a very hot day and experiments in the Explosive Inspectorate's laboratory at Woolwich were able to prove that some of the ingredients became unstable when warmed. [38] Catherine, although badly burnt, was protected by her special clothing and lived. Five years earlier Michael Mahoney had had to identify his daughter's body but this time he was spared that harrowing task.

MARTINI HENRY

After 1900 the Robson site is marked on some maps as 'Martini Henry ... Managing Director Watson Fogge'. Alexander Henry was a Scottish gunsmith whose rifling design had been combined with the Martini loading system and manufactured for military use at Enfield. Henry himself had died in 1900 so it is unlikely that he himself would have been in Greenwich – perhaps the works was used to make ammunition for non-military rifles made to his designs.

After 1900 The Blenheim Engineering company took over part of the Robson site which bordered on to the

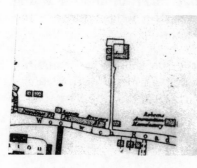

South Metropolitan Gas Works land. They also made fireworks and an accident there in 1902 was reported to the Explosives Inspectorate.

The Firework factory shown on a contemporary map.

13. SMALL INDUSTRY

The housing around Pelton Road, built throughout the nineteenth century, was infilled with small work-shops. On the area to the south of the marsh industries moved into two main areas – along the riverside in Banning and Derwent Streets and at the top of Blackwall Lane in Bellot Street and the area around it. Other industries spread down Blackwall Lane to form a small enclave in the centre of the Peninsula – soon to be sandwiched between riverside industry on the west bank and the great gas works.

One of the longest lasting of East Greenwich indus-tries was among these small sites at the back of the riverside wharves in Derwent Street. James Ashbridge had a forge and smith's shop there before 1870 and a hundred years later his successors, by now 'motor body builders', were still on site.

BANNING STREET AND DERWENT STREET

There were all sorts of 'back street' industries in among the houses. In 1900 there was a sign writer in Banning Street and inevitably the scrap trade, in the shape of George Bischlager, metal dealer and later, as Ernest R. Birdseye, General Dealer. There is just the suspicion that the Greenwich Iron Works of 1900 could have been just another rag and bone man.

The Greenwich Iron Works were joined by another metal trade - the grander sounding Saeculonia Bronze Co. in Derwent Street.

PELTON ROAD

Some small industries seem to have operated from people's homes - an example was 'Walter Cooper, patentee of Steam Traps'. Did he manufacture the 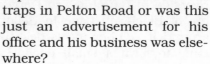 traps in Pelton Road or was this just an advertisement for his office and his business was else-where?

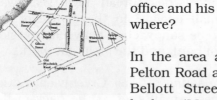

In the area at the far west of Pelton Road at its junction with Bellott Street, George Brown had a 'Mustard Mill' in the 1870s. Small mills that undertook small scale grinding of spices were not unknown in quite ordinary streets - in the 1970s a small mill of this nature was still operating in what looked like a residential front room just off the Walworth Road near the Elephant and Castle. By the 1900s this had become the Kent Forage Mills - a title implying a far grander establishment than Pelton Road can ever have supported. Another such grand sounding works was Richard Gubbins' India Rubber Works; later known as the 'Hammac Rubber Syndicate'.

Many of these small back street industries under-took a service function. There was always a need for wooden barrels – fulfilled by a William Neale who had a cooperage in the otherwise residential Pelton Road and another, William Armstrong, operated nearby in Bellot Street.

The making of traditional wooden barrels was a simple enough process, albeit needing a high level of skills from the cooper himself. The process needed carpentry tools and lots of water but not much space. In the 1980s a cooper like this could be seen at work in the back streets of Bermondsey, unno-ticed by local people who took him and his trade for granted.

BELLOT STREET

The Bellot Street area also supported a pattern maker, John A. Clarke and some small scale metal works, like, in 1903 William Harrod, a brass founder. Another similar works was Flavell, Butler, Montgomery, and Churchill a small engineering firm based in Bellott Street with apparently no relation-ship to the more famous Flavell Electrical Co.

One of the more unlikely trades to be found in the area was the manufacture of manure by a Henry Howard and a Bridge Stondon, who had a 'Manure Works' in an area known as 'Spring Gardens'. This was on the north side of Old Woolwich Road, directly opposite today's Duke of Wellington Public House and right in the middle of the main housing develop-ment. The works included an engine house and was clearly operating on a considerable scale. It must have been very smelly and its existence in the middle of George Smith's careful residential development is astounding. It is probably no coincidence that it was very short-lived.

In the central section of the Peninsula – at the point where today the motorway crosses Blackwall Lane a number of small companies had a precarious existence. In particular there was a succession of small ammunition works in this area

BLACKWALL LANE

The United Lamp Black Works was situated in the middle of the Peninsula. In 1930 ten inhabitants of Tunnel Avenue forced an action against pollution caused by this factory – and at the same time implied that Greenwich Council was negligent, despite surveys by the Sanitary Inspector over a period of ten years.

Mr. Webb had a 'dining rooms' at 159 Tunnel Avenue and he complained of the black specks coming from the factory. He pointed out that fans and ventilators at the factory were defective. He described how he made pastry for a steak pudding and found it full of specks. Customers who tried to eat the pudding, said ' *Hi Governor. What do you call this? Got a sweep knocking about here?* ' [39]

In the twentieth century a small paint industry grew up alongside the Lamp Black Works. Stevenson and Davies, were succeeded by A.E.D.G.Gay, at the Blackwall Lane site.

SAW MILLS AND MAHOGANY

At the top of Blackwall Lane Lister's Saw Mills were in operation from the start of the twentieth century and Greenwich Sawmills Ltd. were on Imperial Wharf for many years. This small woodworking industry was supplemented by an American company which had a short lived works in Greenwich from 1904, Segar Emery.

George D.Emery was an American involved in Nicaraguan mahogany. For unknown reasons he decided to open a London branch in 1904 in conjunction with Samuel Segar. Emery was an important industrialist in the United States and his dealings in Nicaragua are said to have had far more to do with politics than mahogany.[40] Something small in a Greenwich context may in fact be a large operation on the international scene.

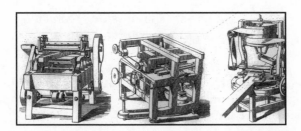

Machinery used by the National Company for Boat Building by Machinery. From right to left – Plane-surfacer, Machine for bearding and rebating, Machine for giving the plank its exterior and interior finish.

14. SHIPS AND SHIPBUILDING

The river is the single most important factor in determining the industries of the Greenwich Peninsula. Boats had been used and maintained all along the riverside since time immemorial. Most of them were barges and lighters – and East Greenwich was to become home to some stunningly successful sailing barges.

Larger ships were built here too, but with less success. By the 1860s Lower Thamesside *'constituted the greatest shipbuilding area in the world'.* [41]

It is an industry that has persisted until relatively recently – and has ended only with a great of reluctance on the part of some boat builders.

BAY WHARF

The riverbank area now known as Bay Wharf was developed by Morden College rather later than the sites to its immediate south. It was once known as

'Horseshoe Breach' and it was probably formed by a break in the sea wall which was made before 1620. Its shape meant that it was ideal for boat building slips - and that is what it became when Morden College leased it to an American in 1864 for his National Company for Boat Building by Machinery.

Small boats had been made up and down the River for millennia - but never boats like this! Small boats were needed for many reasons - with as many designs as purposes. Nathan Thompson wanted to build boats, thousands of them, and they had to be all identical to each other.

THE WOODEN NUTMEG

Thompson came from New York where he had been a marine engineer for the previous nineteen years. In 1859 his boat building system had been examined by the US Navy Department. Their report showed that he had made it possible to cut the time and manpower needed to build small boats - but that all the boats had to be identical.

Four years later Thompson came to England. A visitor to the works described the machinery as '*practical.... expeditious and economical*' but drew attention to the manufacture of wooden nutmegs in New England.[42]   A wooden nutmeg is sometimes used to describe someone from Connecticut with dishonest intentions. Thompson soon had a number of backers - chief of them was Colonel Sykes, MP, Chairman of the East India Company. His technique

*'Machine for bending and giving the ribs and giving the
ribs their proper curvature' used by the National Company for Boat Building by Machinery. From Illustrated
London News.*

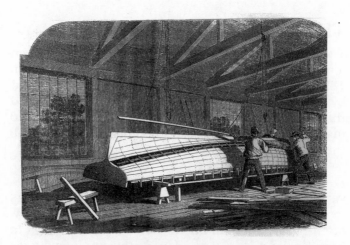

*Putting the parts together on the Assembling
Form. from 'Illustrated London News.'*

was to invite prominent people to a demonstration and ask them to sign a document to say how impressed they were. As a result the Company prospectus included recommendations from an astonishing number of important people, including two Dukes.

Thompson claimed that 25,000 new small boats were needed every year in Britain and he would supply a quarter of them. He knew that '*a quarter of all the ships' boats built in the United Kingdom were for use in Thames built ships*'.[43] Since his new works would be surrounded by large shipyards he could not fail to sell his boats. He said that if only one fifth of all the boats needed in Great Britain were made by the company then they would make a profit. His system depended on a series of fourteen machines, all steam driven. Boats were built round a central 'assembling form' which held everything together in the right place. This machinery needed a very large cash investment but he said that labour costs would be only a quarter of that normally required. Cheapness meant that independent fisherman and others without access to large amounts of capital could afford to buy new boats more often.

Thompson set about making Horseshoe Breach fit for use by building a causeway and putting a boom across the bay. He faced the river wall with stone. New buildings were to be '*proper brick built structures*' by agreement with Morden College. It would be nice to be able to say that Thompson's automated manufacture methods were a great success but, predictably, the company went out of business in its first year. Thompson and his boat building system disappeared from the Thames. He had registered his patents all over the world – and it is a matter of speculation where he went next.

Happily much of the capital Thompson had invested had turned Bay Wharf into a practical ship building area – and that is what it became for the next forty years.

MAUDSLAY SON AND FIELD

In 1864 a different company took over the new slips and boat yard at Horseshoe Breach. They began to extend the slips to take larger craft and by October they had already built a ship - *The Lady Derby*.

The new occupants were the long established and world famous, Maudslay Son and Field, who wanted to expand their flourishing marine engine business. Henry Maudslay had been born in Woolwich and trained under Marc Brunel. His Lambeth works is famous for many engineering innovations - some of which included marine engines.   Henry Maudslay had died in 1831 but the firm was continued under his sons. The East Greenwich site was fitted up so that work could be transferred from Lambeth and it seems likely that this included some of their marine engine building. They also made boilers in Greenwich from 1872. Maudslay were, of course, famous for their marine engines which they had been making since the early years of the nineteenth century.

It is however very difficult to know which, if any, of these engines were made in Greenwich. During the period after 1864 they built engines for a number of

Launch of the Lady Derby

famous liners and battleships – but were they made in Greenwich?

THE LADY DERBY

On what the *Kentish Mercury* saw as a *'great day for East Greenwich'* the first ship, launched in October 1865, was the Lady Derby - named after the wife of the then Prime Minister. She was a screw collier - purpose built to *'Henwood's patent dynamical principles' for the General Iron Screw Collier Co.'* - meaning that she was meant to carry coal. A dampener was put on the proceedings when Daniel Fitzpatrick, one of the partners in the firm, died the day before the launch - an event that almost led to its cancellation. It meant however that at the 'sumptuous luncheon', which followed, all toasts were cancelled except *'success to the new ship'*.[44] The Sultan of Turkey, one of Maudslay's customers, was present at the launch.

Fitzpatrick's death was bad luck, and bad luck was to stay with the Maudslay shipyard for a long time.

HALLOWEEN AND BLACKADDER

In 1870 two iron sailing clippers, *Halloween* and *Blackadder*, were built alongside each other at Greenwich. They were commissioned by John Willis – the ship owner who later commissioned *Cutty Sark*. Like her, they were probably intended to be fast, showy ships. Such glamorous ships, with a great cloud of sail, received a lot of press coverage. There is just the faintest suspicion that they were built on the cheap.

HALLOWEEN

Halloween's delivery to her new owners was very much delayed because of lawsuits about fitness. Once ready she sailed from Shanghai to London in *the wonderful time of 69 days*' on her maiden voyage. She was unusually fast in light winds because of her raked masts – and *'exceedingly fast'* otherwise. She is said to have closely resembled *Cutty Sark* but was unable to make the same twenty-four hour runs. *Halloween* was on the whole a success.

BLACKADDER

Blackadder never equalled *Halloween's* time although she was well known as a very fast ship. She began badly and went on badly. It was even said of her that she was *'built I' th' eclipse and rigged with curses dark'*[45] She was built to the highest requirements at Lloyds but it was found during her fitting out that there was a problem in her construction and a remedy was used which only caused more trouble. During her first voyage there were numerous problems – which became a disaster when she lost her mast in mid-Atlantic. A series of collisions and accidents followed.

She returned to London in July 1871 to find that, because of the bodged repair, her insurers would not pay out. A more successful trip to Shanghai followed – in this she broke the record time between Deal and Shanghai - but her crew was then transferred to the brand new *Cutty Sark*. *Blackadder* continued with voyages to the China Seas in which she continued her career of damage and collisions. In 1899 she was sold to a Norwegian owner and was eventually wrecked at Bahia, in Brazil, in 1905.

BESSEMER AND SEA SICKNESS

Henry Bessemer commissioned an experimental boat from Maudslay while his abortive steel works was on an adjacent site. He suffered greatly from seasickness and designed a boat in which the passenger accommodation would hang free of any rolling motion. Maudslay was asked to build a 'small steamer' in which his experimental cabin could be fitted. Unfortunately while it was being built he changed his plans and the boat was disposed of. Bessemer, who clearly by then had enough money to do exactly what he liked, built a full-scale model boat in his back garden in Denmark Hill.

DESPATCH

Much of Maudslay's work in later days was in the construction of small naval vessels. For example in 1869 *HM Tank Vessel Despatch* was launched - the second vessel built by Maudslay for service in the King William Victualling yard at Portsmouth, the other being, *The Pelter*.

Maudslay Son and Field went into liquidation in 1900. By 1904 Bay Wharf site was in other use and later the barge slips now on site were built as a barge repair facility for Humphrey and Grey.

WILLIAM COURTNEY

In the 1860s there was another shipbuilder on Greenwich Marsh – William Courtney, located near Ordnance Wharf. He may have had a partner in Mr. Henworth, associated with Maudslay in the Lady Derby. Although Courtney described himself as a shipbuilder there is no evidence that he ever built any ships, in fact from the archive record, his career lurched from one disaster to another.

Courtney lived in Lee Terrace and his father may have been a Surveyor of Shipping. In the early 1860s he moved to a site partly owned by Trinity Hospital and partly by Morden College. Morden College, as usual, made conditions about construction. Courtney seems to have installed a steam engine, built some 'sheds' and some other buildings. He had ceased to pay rent by 1866 and, in due course, an action for possession was taken against him. He fought the action in the courts and eventual possession by the court sheriff was complicated by the fact that the bailiffs were unable to work out from the boundary markers the exact extent of his land. They reported that it was in a 'disgraceful state'. By the 1870s the remaining debts were written off and a fire finished off any buildings that remained. Courtney himself had died in 1869.

This appears to be a straightforward financial failure, but an unexplained incident remains. In 1892, when Courtney had been dead for thirteen years, Morden College recorded that '*Two clergymen*' had been in touch '*in regard of settlement of fraud on the Courtney Estate*'. Perhaps we will never know.

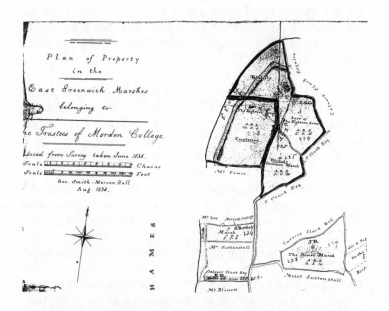

A plan from Morden College with alterations which show the Blakeley and Courtney sites. With kind permission of the Trustees of the Martin Collection.

STOCKWELL AND LEWIS

Yet another shipbuilder found a site on Ordnance Wharf in the 1860s. In October 1868 Alfred Lewis and John Stockwell moved in. They had an existing ship building works at Bow Creek where they had built the steam yacht 'Wolverine' for Major Brandram, the Rotherhithe and Shad Thames industrial chemist, who lived in Blackheath.

Lewis and Stockwell applied to have the riverside footpath blocked off through Ordnance Wharf, despite some protest from the Greenwich vestry about loss of ancient rights, this went ahead. The footpath was to be stopped in order that a dry dock could be built. It was to be part of a ship building yard of about two acres which also contained punching and rolling sheds, a blacksmiths, saw mills, and other factory buildings. The site covered about 3 acres with a 400-foot frontage on the River. The 400' foot dry-dock could take ships of 2,000 to 3,000 tons and the works employed around 300 men.

The works undertook ship repair work although some shipbuilding may been done - they are reputed to have built six 'steamers' for Brazil there. External painting of ships and general repairs were carried out in the dock. Lewis claimed that 'Cape ships' and 'P&P Steamers' were repaired there and needed a 24-hour turn round period. More delicate work was done on 'gentleman's yachts' and it was claimed that this included a vessel belonging to W.H.Smith - bookseller and First Lord of the Admiralty. One repair in the dock was described as replacing the stern post of a large ship that had hit a rock.

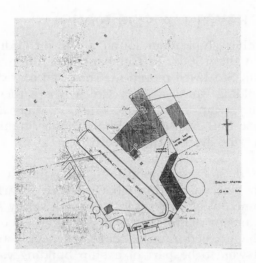

Plan of Blackwall Point Dry Dock.
Kind permission National Gas Archive.

Before 1880 John Stockwell was replaced in the company by Samuel Hyam. Neither Hyam nor Lewis lived in Greenwich. Both came from the Westbourne Grove area of west London. Hyam seems to have been a lawyer used by Lewis to negotiate a price for the site when the South Metropolitan Gas Works was planned to be built on the adjacent site. In this context Hyam claimed that ship repairs would be incompatible with the smell of gas '*the prevailing wind will carry coal dust onto the ships. It would only be injurious so far as the dust is concerned*'.[46]

Hyam and Lewis asked for compensation if the gas

works was built. In due course and following a House of Lords enquiry, the Gas Company was required to compulsory purchase the dry dock and its associated works in 1882.

For many years to come the dock was to prove a problem for the Gas Company.

PASCOE AND WRIGHT

The South Metropolitan Gas Company records show that the gas company leased Blackwall Point dry dock to a ship repair company, Pascoe and Wright in 1881. They also report that in mid-1884 the cassion collapsed and damaged a vessel - the *Richmond Hill* – under repair at the time. As a result of the accident Pascoe and Wright were unable to pay the rent and left.

THE DRY DOCKS CORPORATION OF LONDON

After the *Richmond Hill* incident South Metropolitan Gas Co. rented the dock to a ship repair company, the Dry Docks Corporation of London. Three years later they agreed to arrange a mortgage in order to sell the dock to them. Within a year the Dry Dock Corporation had defaulted on this mortgage and so the gas company decided to dispose of the dock by auction in 1889. No bids were received and the gas company was forced to take the dock back and to look for a new company to operate it.

JOHN STEWART AND SONS

In 1892 The South Metropolitan. Gas Co. began to rent Blackwall Point Dry Dock to John Stewart whose Blackwall ironworks was nearby. They specialised in engines for tugs and steamers. The agreement between the two companies was for only three years because the gas company speculated that when the Blackwall Tunnel was built things would change and they could either ask for more rent or dispose of the dock completely. At the end of the three years however they were obliged to relet it at the same rent. In 1900 they finally sold it to Stewarts for £10,000 down and £12,000 in seven years time.

The gas company must have thought they were now rid of the dry dock but by 1910 Stewarts were in financial trouble and the gas company had to buy it back from the liquidators who asked for £21,000 – only £1,000 less than it had been sold for. It then seems to have passed into the ownership of the Port of London Authority from whom the gas company eventually bought it back again in 1925 for £30,000. They turned it into a reservoir, keeping the capstans and some decorative features.

In 1928 the dock caisson was again broken away in a storm but the dock remained in use as a reservoir until it was filled in some time after the second world war. A capstan from it remained on the riverside as a commemorative feature for many years and after the gas works closed was discovered mouldering among the long grass and dereliction. It was rescued by the Museum in Docklands.

15. SAILING BARGES

Somewhere between the nineteenth and twentieth centuries the massive Thames ship building industry moved, or was sent, to the North of England and Scotland. It was cheaper to build iron ships there because of the easy availability of coal and iron. Boat building - small boats, barges and lighters - has never really gone away. Undoubtedly the most common has been the ubiquitous Thames lighter – an open, unpowered barge.

Despite the clippers, *Blackadder* and *Halloween,* East Greenwich had never been famous for shipbuilding. Ironically it was after the big ships left that East Greenwich boat building came into its own. For several years at the start of the twentieth century a number of thoroughbred sailing barges were built here which went on to win prizes and many admirers.

BARGE BUILDERS BEFORE 1880

There were several barge builders on the Peninsula

before 1880 but little is known about them. In the 1800s barges were very common. Every factory and works needed them because they were the main means of haulage on the River and as common as lorries are in the late twentieth century. Barge repairers must have had a lot in common with motor repairers – dirty, unglamorous and with a bad reputation. They fitted into the holes and corners which others left and undertook a trade which everyone needed and at the same time disregarded.

The earliest boat builder recorded on the Greenwich Peninsula is a Mr. Cruden. He caused a great deal of nuisance to Morden College tenants for some years. His work was done on the foreshore in the area where Charles Holcombe wanted to embank the River and build wharves. Cruden was not paying rent- and, apparently, did not intend to do so. He also blocked what had been osier beds with his barges. Holcombe reported this to Morden College and when James Soames took over part of the site he agreed to take the problem on. The matter was decided at Maidstone assizes and Mr. Cruden left.

Another barge builder from the 1860s was a James West whose barge house was alongside the Sea Witch Pub. He was either part of, or next to, a barge yard belonging to George Bullock who also had a 'grid iron for ships' further north, but advertised his services as a ship repairer and timber merchant from an address in Thames Street, Greenwich.

Augustus Edmonds leased part of the Blakeley site from Morden College before 1880 for a barge building yard. There must have been much more to

Edmonds than appears from the brief note about his tenancy because he was clearly a rich man. In 1868 he had leased a very large and important house, which once stood in Westcombe Hill on the site of the present day Broadbridge Close. Did he have a business somewhere else?

There are others who have not been traced; Henry Pearmaine and perhaps Hughes who probably built the one East Greenwich barge still afloat – *Orinoco* - which in the 1990s could be found at Hoo Marina on the Medway.

BARGES UNDER SAIL

The most famous barges were the red sailed bulk haulage carriers of the Thames tideway and beyond - called 'sprit sail' because of the special arrangement of mast and sail which allowed them to be worked with a minimal crew. Bob Roberts, a well known authority on them, described his moment of conversion when he saw *Reminder* – '*a grey steel barge.. gawky and awkward*' leaving the Albert Dock with '*a fluttering of white canvas and within a matter of moments she was a cloud of sail*'.[47] '*Reminder*' is still in sail and berthed at Maldon.

River workers and bargemen lived in a world that was a rather different shape to that of landsmen. It covered the River – went up to Brentford then down to the Estuary and well beyond. It was a closed, rather elite, world. There was the River, and then there was everyone else. The two didn't really mix.

The barge trade represented what was important about commerce on London River – they carried dirty, everyday, cargoes. Tar from Aylesford to Dunkirk; 'Spent' oxide from Portsmouth Gas Works to the glassworks at Rouen; timber loaded in the Surrey Docks; grain for the mills at Ipswich; cement to everywhere and anywhere; scrap iron from Goole; coal to Wapping; flour to Guernsey and granite road chippings back. They went on and on.

The Thames Barge design had evolved over many centuries but was refined during the nineteenth century. In many ways they were very modern. One barge still in sail in the 1990s – but not Greenwich built – is *Xylonite*. She was built in 1926 as a bulk acid carrier and named *BX* after her owners' main product, the first plastic, British Xylonite.

CITY OF LONDON

At least one prize-winning sailing barge, *The City of London*, was built at East Greenwich before James Piper arrived. Barge races began in 1862 but the builders of contestants are not noted for the first years. '*City of London*' had been built in 1880 and came second in the 1881 Topsail class. She won the race in 1887 and was still racing ten years later.

Sailing barges are essentially glamorous craft. They have the same collectability as tea clippers or the great transatlantic liners! Like the clippers they represent the final moments of working sail during the period when the London river serviced the greatest port in the world. They were largely owned by river haulage companies for whom, through their

Barges in an early race round the Nore Lightship.
From 'Illustrated London News'.

distinctive style, their red sails and their racing
prowess, they provided a living advertisement. Their
status is shown by the names they were given - 'the
famous *Giralda*' was named after the tower of
Seville's cathedral.

PIPER'S

Piper's Wharf is one of the most famous barge
building sites on the River – and the site is still in
use today.   In the early years of the twentieth
century Piper's produced a long line of successful
barges - several of them built to win the annual
barge races. Predominant was 'the famous' *Giralda*
built in 1889 - '*champion of champions*'.

James Richard Piper had been apprenticed to a Greenwich ship owner, William Bromley, and then went to work for Mowlem's in Greenwich. After ten years he opened a barge repair business where he began to build barges to his own designs and through hard work built the firm up.

There were problems with his first site because of the movement of the tide and Piper moved as soon as he could do so to a new wharf, which became known as 'Piper's'. By 1899 he had designed and built the largest 'dumb' barges. His sailing barges too were becoming well known and his order book was full. Piper's had some pretensions above the usual barge and lighter repairers of East Greenwich – advertising themselves from the first as 'Barge and Yacht builders'. In due course James Piper was succeeded by Leonard and, then Malcolm. While they built a wide range of working Thames boats and some pleasure craft but they were rightly most famous for their classic sailing barges.

The earliest barge built at Greenwich by Piper was called, fittingly, *James Piper* - she ended her days as a Chelsea houseboat. She was followed by *Haughty Belle*, *Gerty* and *Ernest Piper* - a few remains of which can still be seen sitting on Medway mud at Bedlam's Bottom, near Sittingbourne. In the early 1900s Piper's were turning out at least one barge a year. These were commissioned, or sold to the river haulage companies.

Goldsmith's of Grays commissioned *Giralda*. Ugly and flat-bottomed, she was built to win the prize money for Victoria's Jubilee year gold cup. She followed this by winning race after race for many years. She had less success as a working barge and a row was to develop as to whether she could cope with the loads of cement, bricks, rubbish or corn - the routine loads of any working barge.

Piper's followed with many other barges and most of them led useful working lives. They still aspired to racing success - a barge of 1904 was called *Surge* (*S*ure yo*U* a*R*e *G*iralda's *E*qual). By the 1930s the annual championships were dominated by East Greenwich barges.

Sailing barge careers and their final fates are recorded in detail by the enthusiasts who follow them. Some Greenwich barges still remain useful, although there is no Piper barge now still sailing. *Leonard Piper* is now a houseboat at Chiswick and *Wilfred* is a Victoria Embankment wine bar.

Piper's built many other vessels at East Greenwich – lighters, motor barges even some launches. In the Second World War they turned out landing craft and 'things of that nature'. For a while, in the 1950s, they specialised in refrigerated craft. They did conversions – in 1981 they converted a 3,000 ton vessel for cable repairers in New Zealand.

Memories of the sailing barges remained with them and for many years the great main mast of *Genesta* stood outside the Greenwich works, as a memento - she had been missing in a storm for four days off

Blyth. The mast was in Greenwich but *Genesta* stayed afloat and went to Guernsey.

SHRUBSALL

Shrubsall was another important Greenwich barge builder. They were an established company with a yard at Ipswich and at Limehouse and also at Sittingbourne. Then, in 1900 Horace Shrubsall rented a piece of land from Morden College – part of the area which was to be later used by the Delta Metal Co. Shrubsall later took over what was to be known as Tunnel Wharf. Shrubsall were established barge builders when they came to Greenwich with a good record of producing effective boats. Their barges were soon to challenge Piper's – in the 1907 race *Veronica* was only two minutes behind *Giralda*. *Veronica* is now lying on the mud at Bedlam's Bottom with all her ribs showing – but her bow boards are preserved in the Dolphin Yard Museum at Sittingbourne. No Greenwich built Shrubsall barge remains active. Sadly, *Vicunia* was burnt out at Maldon only in 1994. *Verona* is said to be in use as a houseboat in Stockholm.

The barge fraternity was proud of its record in the Second World War. Several went over for the Dunkirk landings. *Duchess* was abandoned off Dunkirk in June 1940 where *Valonia* too was lost – although she was discharging tar from Aylesford at Dunkirk when, as her skipper is reported to have said, *'Jerry got there first'*.[48]

NORTON'S

So recently was Norton's yard in work that in the late 1990s odd bits of plank and chain can still be found on the foreshore. Old men from Greenwich Yacht Club say - *'they were from Dick Norton's ....pick up the barge nails'* - all that is left of a skilled and flourishing trade. Norton's lasted into the 1970s and although Dick Norton sold the yard in 1966 he still came down. The yard housed an attractive jumble of old sheds minded by Fred the watchman.

Nortons built sailing barges on the foreshore at Bugsby's Reach. A plan of the riverfront, drawn up for the steel works shows three Nortons – 'R.Norton, Snr' – 'Norton Bros.' and 'Norton Jnr'. None had a wharf but existed on the foreshore with barge blocks

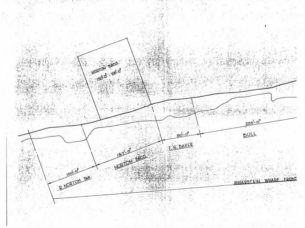

Part of plan showing Nortons' barge yards in front of the Redpath Brown works.

running parallel to the bank. 'R.Norton' alone had a small area inland. Pat O'Driscoll remembered '*There was a little wicket gate in the corrugated iron fence..... Norton had two sheds on the other side, one was for storing tools, nuts, bolts, paint, etc. The other was Fred's living quarters'.*[49]

In 1908 they rebuilt the wrecked *Empress* as *Scudo* and then built *Scout, Scud* and *Serb* from new. *Scud* was a 64-ton vessel, which worked for seventy-three years until she was broken up in Sittingbourne, only in 1980. *Serb*, bigger at 75 tons had a shorter life of only thirty-eight years before she was sunk off the North Foreland in 1954.

BARGES AND BOATS

Barge and boat building has been very tenacious at East Greenwich – so much so that it would be no surprise to walk along the riverside one-day and find something quite large under construction. So resilient was this industry that the Barge Builders Union continued to meet in Greenwich until the early 1980s.

Still to be seen are the disused barge building slips at Bay Wharf built for Humphrey and Grey. In 1908 a Mr. Humphrey had joined several other barge builders at Point Wharf. By 1919 he was in partnership with Mr. Grey, Jnr. and then moved to Bay Wharf where the slips were built. Thomas Hughan replaced him at Point Wharf and remained there for many years.

Joe Jackobaits moved to Point Wharf after Hughan

left it. He had had a business in the Royal Docks and, ousted from there, stayed at Greenwich as long as he could. At Point Wharf he built a number of boats on a special – if makeshift – structure constructed so as to allow pedestrians past. It is instructive to learn that as late as 1987 he was still at work there and can point to some surprisingly large Greenwich built vessels in use on the River and elsewhere today, which were built on the site adjacent to the Dome's building site entrance.

As the Millennium Dome nears completion, next to the smart offices at Ordnance Draw Dock lies a rusting heap of marine artefacts - necessary for the boat building business, since boat builders say that pedestrians on the riverside path obstruct their work if more traditional methods are used. They clearly intend to start again as soon as possible – Dome or not.

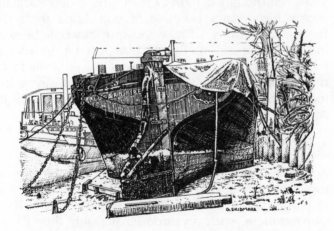

The Leonard Piper in use as a housebarge at Chiswick. Picture by kind permission George Skidmore.

16. RAILWAYS AND DOCKS

Up until the middle of the nineteenth century the main transport link between East Greenwich industries and the rest of the world was the River.

The first railway in London came to Greenwich in 1836 – although it didn't cross Greenwich Park for nearly forty years because of objections from the Royal Observatory. Railways were however becoming an important mode of transport for industrial users as for passengers. If it was not possible to go through the park then the way to get a railway to the industries onto the Greenwich Peninsula was to go round it.

ANGERSTEIN

Angerstein is a name, which keeps cropping up in the East Greenwich area. It originates with the romantic figure of John Julius Angerstein - a Russian financier with mysterious, possibly illustrious, origins. He may well have been the son of the Empress Ann of Russia and a British banker. He spent a long working life in the City of London, regularised Lloyds of London and whose pictures provided the foundation of the National Gallery.

In 1774 Angerstein bought land in Blackheath and built the house which is now Woodlands, Greenwich Local History Library. He had numerous connections within the City of London and political circles. Although Greenwich marsh was a small item in his enormous world of influence, Angerstein, is one of a number of influential people who can be said to have shaped the marsh and its industries. His country home was built to overlook the area of the marsh itself. His area of influence was in the east of the Marsh along Lombard's Wall.

Angerstein owned the area that roughly covers to-day's Westcombe Park. Part of Westcombe Park Road may have been his carriage drive. He, and his family, went on to acquire, by 1856, the whole stretch of land between the River and the Dover Road. Coombe Farm covered much of the lower part of this area with its buildings north of Westcombe Park Station.

John Julius had one son, John, born in 1773 who lived much of the time in Greenwich. He had a large family - the most important members in this context are a younger John Julius (born 1801) and William (born 1812). John Julius himself had died in 1823.

In 1850 John Angerstein must have seen the stretch of land between Blackheath and the River as full of potential. The North Kent railway line was being built through a tunnel, which ran from Blackheath to a point adjacent to his land. On the other side of the River the new Victoria Dock was to have an entrance almost opposite. All that would be needed was a wharf and a connecting railway and good business would be guaranteed.

ANGERSTEIN'S RAILWAY

A railway was planned in 1851 to run on Angerstein's land from the North Kent Railway as it emerged from its tunnel into a chalk pit. The Angerstein line would then go to a riverside wharf. Built on private  land there was no need for an Act of Parliament except for the bridge needed to cross the Lower Turnpike Road between Greenwich and Woolwich. The Act was applied for and passed in May 1851.

The line opened in 1852 but had already been leased to the South Eastern Railway for operation. The spoil removed from the Blackheath/Charlton railway tunnel was used to build the embankment on which the railway goes on its way to the River. It runs parallel with Lombard's Wall - the Tudor flood defence and property marker.

The railway line was, and has remained, entirely a goods line. As industry grew in East Greenwich and Charlton so it grew and was extended. In the 1890s the line was extended right across the Peninsula to enter the gas works via a bridge across Riverway.

ANGERSTEIN WHARF

As industry grew the Angerstein line appears on successive maps with up to fourteen branches fanning out east and west from it to factories and the riverside. In 1925 an article said that goods worth £58,000 were handled in 1859, rising tenfold by the 1920s. The Wharf then handled '*manure, steel rails, fertiliser, coal, coke, stone, sand, flour, slates and timber*'. By 1951 however the 755-foot river frontage with an upper dock '*too small*' for '*present day craft*' was mainly taking petroleum spirit and oil - together with '*Fullers' Earth from Redhill, ... timber, flour, manure, iron and steel, and waste paper*'[50]

In 1999 the wharf handles aggregate - much of which is carried along the old railway line.

THE DOCK THAT NEVER WAS

In the 1850s dock construction was booming in London. Where you had a dock so you had a railway. In the late 1850s plans were made which would have entirely changed the face of the Greenwich Peninsula – there would have been no space for a Dome of any sort! The plans were repeated in the 1880s. There is just the suspicion of hype about them.

Railways were being planned all round the country; some of them were even being built. The Mercer's Company owned a small piece of land to the south of the Peninsula and they recorded approaches in this period from several railway companies who wanted to build over, or near, their land. In December 1852 they, like Morden College, were approached by the South Eastern Railway, in connection with an extension of the Angerstein line and a plan to join it both to Blackwall via a ferry and the Greenwich Railway from London Bridge. This appears to have come to nothing.

In May 1853 the Mercers were approached by the, otherwise unknown, Charlton and Blackwall Railway. It was hinted that docks were actually what were planned. Little more was heard of this plan until 1857 when there was a sudden new departure. An application was made to Parliament for a grand dock to be built on the Greenwich Peninsula.

This story is closely interwoven with Greenwich politics. In this period Greenwich saw an astonishing number of Parliamentary elections and by elections with some lively personalities emerging in the context of even livelier election campaigns – at a time when two members were elected to parliament by Greenwich voters. They included local industrialists, like Peter Rolt, colourful local characters like John Townsend, and David Salomans the first Jew to be elected to Parliament. Another contestant was William Angerstein. Local people and local industrialists threw themselves into this succession of election campaigns – one of the most assiduous was Coles Child. In this context it should be noted that Coles Child was a director of the South Eastern Railway during the 1850s. It might be assumed that the South Eastern Railway was behind the great dock scheme in that the plans name it as the 'Greenwich and South Eastern Docks.' It seems however, like so many others, to have been legally a separate company – which means that any records

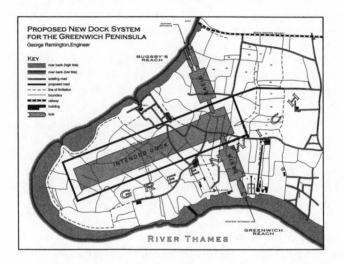

PROPOSED NEW DOCK SYSTEM FOR THE GREENWICH PENINSULA
George Remington, Engineer

KEY
- river bank (high tide)
- river bank (low tide)
- existing road
- proposed road
- line of limitation
- boundary
- railway
- building
- lock

Plan for the Greenwich Dock Scheme. Thanks to Chris Grabham for computer enhancement work.

are difficult, or impossible to trace. Plans of the proposed dock show an enormous scheme which would have taken up most of the land on the Peninsula – the length of the dock was to run north-south down the length of the land. The whole structure was to be in a 'T' shape so that the main north-south dock was met by another at right angles with entrances at Enderbys' Wharf to the west, and the end of what is now Riverway in the east - where it would also have met the Angerstein Railway.

The scheme was noted with approval by the *Kentish Mercury* in 1858 just before yet another election. Their leader writer spoke of the miserable time people were having in Greenwich '*the silence is only broken at intervals by the sepulchral sound of the wheels of an empty omnibus.... even if you see some active pedestrian approaching the public baths, from having nothing else do to, his gloomy countenance renders it doubtful whether he is about to enter for the purposes of ablution or to drown himself*'.

In 1858 the Dock was being presented as part of a package. The North and South Metropolitan Junction Railway would change everything – make travel throughout the capital easy and bring peace and prosperity to Greenwich. At the same time in 1858 another election was under way. In this one of the candidates was William Angerstein who had inherited the land around the Angerstein Railway in Greenwich.'*A Reader*' wrote to the *Mercury* '*At last there seems a chance of poor Greenwich being resuscitated and rising from the ashes. I and others have hailed the advent of the Greenwich and South Eastern Docks*'. The question was of course - where did the candidates for Parliament stand on this issue?

Votes were not secret then and in the run up to any election the *Mercury* was happy to print on its front page lists of names of voters with their voting intentions, week by week, as the election approached. On December 2nd '*Straight*' wrote to them and enquired whether the candidates would '*put their hands in their pockets .. and assist projects*'. The *Mercury's* leader writer was happy to point out that some 40 acres of land which would be needed to build the dock were owned by William Angerstein.

Angerstein was pressed to accept a seat on the Board of the Dock Company – which he refused and it is likely that an acceptance would have led to charges of corruption. Instead he found himself accused in the *Mercury* by Coles Child of not supporting improvements which would benefit Greenwich people – followed by the public announcement that Coles Child would no longer remain on the list of Angerstein's election supporters. In the following week's paper Coles Child asked if Angerstein would be prepared to '*make the Company a present of the land required*'? Needless to say this gift was not forthcoming from Angerstein who went on to lose the election.

A SECOND DOCK SCHEME

After 1859 the issue of the dock scheme went very quiet. It was raised again in the 1860s when proposals were made to extend the railway from Greenwich or Blackheath to Angerstein wharf. Nothing came of any of it.

The dock scheme came up again in the 1880s. Ostensibly it was not put forward by the South Eastern Railway although, as they paid for the parliamentary deposit, it must have had something to do with them. It no longer included a dock along the length of the Peninsula, only the cross head of the 'T' junction. It proved a severe embarrassment to the South Metropolitan Gas Company whose East Greenwich works were then under consideration.

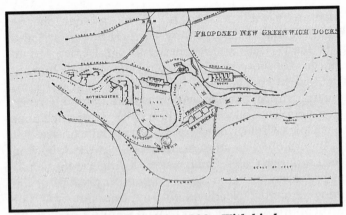

The dock plan of the 1880s. With kind permission of the Trustees of the Martin Collection.

17. COAL AND CHEMICALS

As the nineteenth century progressed so the chemical industry began to come into its own. Many of these chemicals were derived from coal and were the direct result of its increasing use as a source of power. The new gas works set up throughout London from 1811 were, in effect, chemical factories re-processing coal for fuel. One result of this was a vast and increasing pile of waste products – mostly main tar and ammonia – which the gas industry was unable or reluctant to use itself. This role was filled by entrepreneurs who were able to use this waste as a raw material for chemical products. All around East London such works were set up to make unattractive but useful substances. A lot of money was made by some of these industrialists – and East Greenwich was an area to which several of them came.

THE HILLS

Frank Hills bought the tide mill in 1842. He was a

member of an enterprise that involved his father, numerous brothers and their sons. His father, Thomas Hills, was at the Bromley-by-Bow Steam Mills on the River Lea – north of the River -in 1811. There he had taken out a patent for a revolutionary process for making sulphuric acid, or vitriol, using a locally available natural product, pyrites, rather than traditional brimstone. This was an important developments in the chemical industry of the early nineteenth century. Sulphuric acid is a key product in the development of an industrial nation.

Thomas had several sons – most of whom had found chemical works of their own. Arthur, for instance, was at Nine Elms, Wandsworth and on the Isle of Dogs - opposite Greenwich. Henry, managed to live in Blackheath Paragon while his chemical works was in the strange industrial village of Amlwch on the furthermost tip of Anglesey, and his son, Henry Charles, managed the Anglesey Copper Works on the banks of the Tyne in Newcastle. There is every reason to believe that this family network worked closely together as one unit. In the early 1830s Frank Hills rented a chemical works in Deptford from a German chemist, Wilhelm Beneke who had been working on substances to be obtained from gas works ammonia. Frank Hills took both works and ideas over and soon he was looking to expand.

In the 1840s East Greenwich provided large 'greenfield' sites. Both Arthur and Edwin Hills had approached Morden College for a lease in the area, and been refused. It was Frank who eventually moved to the area, buying the old tide mill – *'dilapidated, really just a stack of materials'* in 1845.

By the 1850s the water wheel at the tide mill had been was replaced by a 25-horse power steam engine made by William Joyce whose factory was near Deptford Creek. In the 1840s Frank had made two steam driven road vehicles - but henceforth he was to confine himself to chemicals.

FRANK HILLS

Frank Hills, backed by his brothers, built a large chemical works on the riverside to the north of the old tide mill. He bought tar and ammonia in large quantities from the various gas works in London and

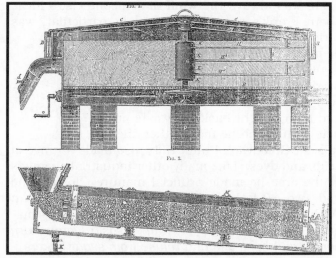

Hills' Improved Apparatus for Purifying gas. From 'The Mechanics Magazine'. A process for cleaning up coal gas was how Frank Hills made a great deal of money.

beyond. There is every indication that his brothers were doing the same at their various works. Frank worked assiduously at Deptford and Greenwich to perfect a chemical process with which he was to make a great deal of money. He won several prizes at the Great Exhibition of 1851 at Crystal Palace for his ammonia salts and 'gas tar'.

Frank also patented a process for the 'purification' of newly made coal gas'. Coal gas, as everyone knows, has a bad smell and in order to make it fit to be burnt for lighting in the home it had to be cleaned up. There was a lot of competition among chemists to perfect a workable process and Frank defended his patent vigorously in interminable court cases. There was always the whiff of someone else's ideas about Frank's patents and this, in particular, was seriously challenged. Using this patent he made a great deal of money through issuing licences to gas companies who used his method – at the same time he sold them the necessary raw materials, and then bought back the waste products with which he made other chemicals. At Greenwich Frank Hills also made a range of acids and dyes. Like many other industrial chemists in the area he made artificial manure - for this he had two 30-ft long steam boilers as well as an 'Archimedean screw' and a bone crusher. This manure was made from '*shoddy - waste leather, dry bones, and bone ash and refuse from sugar bakers*' - and whatever other organic rubbish could be bought cheaply. The whole was then mixed with sulphuric acid and the smell can be imagined (perhaps better if it is not!).

In 1871 Mr. Pink, the Medical Officer of Health for Greenwich, gave 'advice' designed for '*abatement of the nuisance which these works could scarcely have failed to occasion*'.

The wharf alongside the Greenwich works at the end of Riverway was kept very busy. Ships delivered materials from Frank Hills' mines in Spain and Wales. He was a ruthless and unscrupulous businessman but the chemicals he made in his dirty factory were used all over the world. Some of the money he made was invested in heavy engineering.

Across the river from East Greenwich is Bow Creek where the vast engineering and ship building complex of Thames Ironworks turned out liners and flagships for the world's navies - the ship yard where Warrior was built. Frank Hills controlled that, too and it was handed over in due course to his desperately eccentric son, Arnold.

PHOENIX WORKS

Frank Hills died in the 1890s and his two eldest sons also died within a year of him. The Greenwich works, semi-derelict, was sold to the South Metropolitan Gas Co. It was duly modernised and became part of the great East Greenwich Gas Works, having been renamed 'Phoenix Wharf'. Gas works waste products had been the staple raw material of Frank Hills' works for fifty years and now the new gas works incorporated it and made it part of their establishment.

The last memory of chemicals at East Greenwich was an amazing 1950s parabolic building used for

Schedule of Plant and Machinery at the Chemical Works, East Greenwich, referred to in Messrs Ellis & Son's Report of —. January 29th 1895.

Two Elevators with buckets, strap & gear.

A Separator with frame & gear.

Six pair of Crushing Stones.

A Grinding Mill.

An Archimedean Screw.

A Crushing Machine with fly-wheel & bearings.

A pair of Vertical inverted oscillating — Steam Engines by Joyce of Greenwich with cogged fly-wheel, frame & fittings.

A bone crusher with frame & gear.

Two Steam Boilers with setting & — chimney shaft.

The whole of the Shafting, bearings, — riggers, straps, bevil wheels and Running Gear for the above Machinery

Estate Agent's Assessment for Chemical Works equipment 1895 - drawn up to interest potential buyers in the works. Kind permission Maj Wagstaffe.

storage of sulphate of ammonia. It was demolished in the late 1980s, while under consideration for listing, because, the owners said, illicit 'rave parties' were being held there. You can still see it used as a stage or a backdrop in 'pop' videos and plays of the period - film makers loved it!

JOHN BETHELL

Frank Hills had developed chemicals based on gas works ammonia and a gas purification processes. The most bulky waste product from the gas industry was coal tar and there were many attempts in the early nineteenth century to find an economic use for it. One of the most successful processes was that  pioneered in the 1830s by John Bethell. He was a barrister from Bristol and the brother of Lord Chancellor, Richard Bethell. He was to exploit his process on a Morden College owned site on the west bank of Greenwich Peninsula.

In 1848 Bethell patented a way of *'preserving animal and vegetable substances from decay'*. There was a great need to find a way of preserving wood from rot and the Earl of Dundonald had suggested the usefulness of coal tar for this in the 1780s. Other inventors had used other preservatives and other methods; Bethell was to take some elements of each to achieve his object.

One particular need was for a cheap way of preserving wooden ships. The eventual success of Bethell's

172

Improved Wood Pavement Co., advertisement.

process was to lead to the world wide use of wood for such things as railway sleepers and telegraph poles. At Greenwich the works eventually specialised in the manufacture of tar soaked wood block paving.

The process which Bethell developed involved an apparatus first designed in Paris. The dried timber was put on iron bogey frames, run into a strong iron cylinder, and the air pumped out. The preservative solution was then forced in. Although a number of preservatives were specified coal tar was the cheapest and easier to obtain. It was also far safer to use than some of the other recommendations - Kyan's sublimate was poisonous and particularly dangerous. Bethell seems to have either sold his patent to others or licensed them to use it.

There were soon a number of works in East London area which preserved wood using Bethell's methods. The most successful and best known were Burt, Boulton and Haywood whose enormous tar processing plant was based in Silvertown on the Essex bank of the Thames.

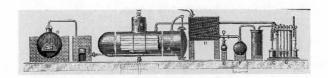

High pressure creosoting cylinder. From
G.Lunge. 'Coal Tar and Ammonia'

Bethell himself set up in business with a tar distillery in Battersea in 1845. He soon expanded with
a chemical works at Bow Common, and another near
Blackwall Point on a site leased from Morden College. His first approach to Morden College had been
as early as 1839 when he asked for the use of a piece
of rough ground. He gave his address as Mecklen-
berg Square - built by the Greenwich Hospital Estates surveyor, Joseph Kaye. His Greenwich works
was soon underway and coal tar was purchased in
bulk from the Imperial Gas Company works at St.
Pancras and Haggerston.

Other chemicals were made at Greenwich - both
sulphuric acid and alum were made on site. Like
Frank Hills Bethell took an interest in gas purification methods.

The Greenwich works remained in operation for
many years. After Bethell's death in the 1870s his
wife Louisa retained ownership – although she lived
in Bath while professional managers ran the company from an address in King William Street, City of
London. In the 1880s the works was transferred to
the Improved Wood Pavement Company in which the
Bethell family remained involved.

OTHER CHEMICAL COMPANIES

Frank Hills and John Bethell represent two sides of
the chemical industry based on gas works waste
products. There were several other works at East
Greenwich involved in this trade. There were others
who ran manure works – some used the same sort of
waste materials as Frank Hills and others were
involved in the South American guano trade.

Many of these industries had links both with government and with the banking and finance sectors of the City of London. The guano trade is a clear case where financiers linked with interests in South America. There is considerable evidence of some South American interests in the Hills' industrial empire.

FORBES ABBOTT

James Forbes and John Abbott were specialists in ammonia based products – sulphate of ammonia was also used as an agricultural fertiliser - James Forbes had patented a number of such ammonia based products. Like several others the firm specialised in buying waste ammonia from the gas industry. Forbes and Abbott had previously been based at Iceland Wharf, Old Ford, in Hackney. In 1889 they moved from their site on Ordnance Wharf to Sussex Wharf – between the tar paving factory and the old Ransome stone works – and for some years operated from both sites. For a while the partnership included John Hare Lennard, from the Wills Tobacco family. They later became the Standard Ammonia Co.

GUANO AND MANURE

At Ordnance Wharf was the Biphosphated Manure Co. It seems to have been owned by Christopher Weguelin, a banker and Trustee of Morden College and a waiver was issued by the College in this instance.

It was not unknown for bankers to be involved in the South American guano trade – Anthony Gibbs is a well-known example. Biphosphated Guano seems to have closed when the gas works opened.

Mockford 'Ordnance' Manure Works moved to Ordnance Wharf in 1873. They had come from the City of London, via Deptford, where they had been in the 'artificial manure' trade since at least the 1860s. They used South American guano, 'shoddy' - waste from fabric manufacture along with sulphate of ammonia.

East Greenwich chemical works shown on a map drawn up by a G.Ballard as part of a pollution report for the Local Government Board, 1870

The sulphate was probably bought from local gas works. Mockford also used 'mineral phosphates' - a trade on the fringe of the extractive industries. At Ordnance Wharf these materials were turned into fertiliser with the aid of sulphuric acid, also made on-site. The process of manufacture led to '*corrosive vapours*' and Edward Ballard, who inspected the site for the Local Government Board,   said '*the stench when these mixings are going on is simply intolerable*'.

Manufacture of 'artificial' manure was an important industry on Thameside in the last century. There were other such works on Greenwich Marsh. In Deptford a most important breakthrough had been made with the development of superphosphates by John Bennett Lawes, and Frank Hills used a similar process at his works in Riverway.   All of these processes used up waste materials from other industries- a useful task but one which meant that a lot of smelly items were stored in the area.

BRIQUETTES

The manufacture of cheap fuel from mixtures of broken coal and dust together with tar was common in the nineteenth century. Although it was not really a chemical industry it was a way of using up gas works waste tar and coal dust from anyone who had any – and stands between chemicals and coal based fuel systems. One such on the Greenwich Peninsula was the Wylam Steam (or Patent) Fuel Co. Although it might be assumed that the name 'Wylam' related to the coal mining district in the North East of England, in fact it seems to be the name of the factory owner - William Wylam who had taken out three patents in the early 1840s for machinery with which to make artificial fuel.

Wylam's firm had previously been in Thames Street, Greenwich, and in 1847 obtained a lease from Morden College for a site on the Marsh. It must be said that a year later they had their supplies of coal tar cut off by their suppliers, the Gas Light and Coke Co., for non payment of bills so they were probably not very prosperous. Despite this setback they were in a position to expand to a larger site in the mid-1860s – and the cause of complaint when they blocked the barge roads outside their wharf.

Sign advertising Improved Wood Pavement Co. Photograph with kind permission by Tim Smith

18. COAL FIRED POWER

THE GAS WORKS

In the mid nineteenth century the coal trade was at its height. Ships from the north east of England and Scotland poured into the Thames. Coal came into the wharves on the Peninsula for all sorts of reasons – some of it was used as a the source of the raw materials for chemical plants, but the main use was to fuel the boilers of the steam engines which began to provide power for the new factories. After 1880 coal was used to supply centralised power plants – like gas works, and later on electrical power stations.

The South Metropolitan Gas Works grew to dominate the Greenwich Peninsula - it was built in the 1880s and was thus a late comer, sited on an area hitherto unused for industrial purposes. It was also very 'modern' – no gas works has been built in London since. It was the new, 'super', works through which the South Metropolitan Gas Company hoped to show the world what it could do.

George Livesey. From: A Century of Gas in South London.

GEORGE LIVESEY

The South Metropolitan Gas Company dated from the late 1820s and had been started by a group of fairly dubious characters in the Old Kent Road. From the 1840s it was managed by members of the Livesey family, first Thomas, and then his son George. By the 1880s George was Chairman of the company – but as a fourteen year old in the 1840s he had begun as an office boy in the Old Kent Road gas works. The building of East Greenwich was to be the pinnacle of his ambitions - simply to be the best in the world.

George Livesey seems to have had no formal education. His childhood in the Old Kent Road left him with fond memories of local people and those who worked for his father. He signed the 'pledge' of temperance in his early teens along with a group of other young workers and, through them, began to attend prayer meetings. At the age of seventeen he attended the first meeting of the London Band of Hope. Temperance was to become his 'other' career and George maintained a lifetime close association with bodies like the Lord's Day Observance, and the Good Templars. Somewhere along the line he picked up ideas from Christian Socialists, co-operators, and most significantly the Italian patriot, Mazzini.

Charging a Retort. A team of workers loads coal into a retort where it will be distilled to make gas From 'Illustrated London News'.

A gas works may not seem the best ground from which to launch a crusade – but George was generally unstoppable. He was clever, good at everything he did, and could never resist a good cause - which ranged from the minutiae of gas works equipment up to grand schemes on the organisation of society itself.

By the 1870s George Livesey had moved the gas company on to the national stage. Through his negotiating coups South Metropolitan had taken control of a number of other local gas companies thus gaining a near monopoly in the area.

In the 1860s the two biggest gas companies in North London had both built large out-of-town works to provide bulk supply and enable them to close down small uneconomic works. Livesey decided that it was high time South Metropolitan did the same - but better - and in the early 1880s the site on the marsh was chosen.

BUILDING THE GAS WORKS

The new gas works was different to the industries which had already come to the Peninsula. As a large public utility, albeit a private company, it had a direct relationship with Parliament and the local authorities. It was not so concerned with any restrictions that Morden College, or other landlords, might impose, and it was big and powerful enough to impose itself on the area around it.

The Gas Company cleared the Parliamentary permission to build the works on 140 acres of in December

View of the South Metropolitan Co. Gasworks, East Greenwich, c. 1920. This picture is clearly of an impossible view. The two gasholders appear to almost on the riverbank, yet today the motorway and Amylum's Tunnel Refineries stand between the still existing gas holder and the river! The picture gives, however, a fine view of the gasworks with the site of Frank Hills' chemical works in the right hand foreground. From 'A Century of Gas in South London'.

1880. Discussions were already underway with the local authority on the new plant and its layout. It had been agreed that the purifying plant, thought to be the smelliest part of the works, should be placed on the northern most tip of Blackwall Point. This would ensure that smells were kept from Greenwich, while wafting over the Isle of Dogs.

There were a number of objections to their plans - Coles Child's executors wanted to build housing, as did Mrs. Fryer, another landowner. The owners of the dry dock on Blackwall Point claimed that the smell would damage the high-class paintwork they said they were doing. Parliament made some requirements before the works could be built - one was that they rebuild the river wall on the eastern bank, and provide Ordnance Draw Dock. The public footpath round the riverbank was closed.

None of this pleased 'waterside people' who continued to cause 'difficulty' by insisting on their old rights of way. Docwra, the gas company's contractors, dealt with this by placing '*a gang of men*' to '*divert this traffic*'. Building work began very slowly. The contractors found access to the site difficult, describing it as '*a cul de sac - and approaches thereto were not inviting*'. Most of the site on which the gas works was to be built, in the centre of the marsh, was '*market gardens of poor quality*'. The builders were constantly reminded of this by the '*sprouting of rhubarb*' throughout the site. Other reminders of the rural past were a few remaining cows which lived in a shed which '*age had rendered rotten and insecure*'.

Others who thought they might have rights in the area were the gypsies for whom it was a *'happy dumping ground'*. With them the contractors were in a *'constant state of warfare'*. During one such running battle, Joseph Tysoe, the future works manager, only escaped serious injury when his assistant intercepted a heavy iron bar aimed at his head.

As work progressed, Docwra brought on site *'extraordinarily powerful pumping apparatus'* and took borings to discover the state of the ground. Barge after barge came loaded with clinker and heavy rubbish to use as infill, but it took *'a vast amount of effort to make a sensible impression on this wilderness'*.

Slowly the works took shape. *'Looming vast against the sky is the skeleton of the great holder'*. This is the holder still to be seen today alongside the Blackwall tunnel approach road. It was thought it would *'darken the sky like a mountain of iron'*. The jetty too was taking shape, sinking as it was built. It was reported that it was *'allowed to go as far as it would'* until it became *'as firm as a rock'*.[51]

East Greenwich gas works became world famous, and was once seen as an example of everything that was progressive in British industry. It must be ironic that in the 1990s we are looking at the gas works site in just the same way as its builders did.

THE GAS HOLDERS

Ever since the gas works came to the Peninsula in the 1880s the structure which dominates the landscape has been the giant gasholder. For most of the time its even bigger neighbour stood alongside it. At twelve million cubic feet capacity, East Greenwich No.2 Gasholder was the biggest in the world when it was built in 1892. Two flying lifts were destroyed by an 1917 explosion and never replaced. No.1. which still stands, is slightly older and smaller – small, in the sense that it was only surpassed by its companion. George Livesey believed in maximising both economy of construction and greatest storage capacity for ground area. The development of his ideas can be seen in its' predecessor holders still standing at the Old Kent Road gas works site.

The holders were built without decoration as a symbol of all that was modern and progressive in British industry. The observer was expected to see them and be impressed, not only with their size but with their rationality.

CHANGE

For George Livesey the works was to be more than just another gas supply factory but was to embody the ideals, which he had cherished from boyhood. Within a few years of its opening a dramatic episode in industrial relations was to change both George Livesey and the South Metropolitan Gas Company in a fundamental manner.

In the late 1880s London was changing. Arguments about the government of London had led to the abolition of the Metropolitan Board of Works and, in late 1889, the election of the first London County Council. Ideas about public ownership of gas were being expressed- something which, naturally, Livesey did not approve of.

THE GREAT STRIKE OF 1889

1889 was the year of the great Dock Strike and the 'new unions'. There had been trade unions in the gas industry since the 1830s and a bitter dispute in 1872 had led to legislation that made strike action illegal for gas workers . In the late 1880s Will Thorne and others began to organise gas workers north of the river on the issue of the eight-hour shift system.

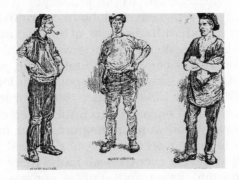

Three gas workers in 1889. From
'Illustrated London News.'

The story of the 1889 strike has often been told. Negotiations proceeded with Will Thorne's new union on a London wide basis but Livesey was determined that 'outsiders', as he termed the union, should not have any power in 'his' works.

Following what he described as a visionary episode on Telegraph Hill in Nunhead Livesey instigated a profit sharing scheme amongst the South Metropolitan. workforce. In this, and in the events that followed, it is sometimes difficult to reconcile Livesey, the deeply religious temperance worker, with the draconian industrialist. The Gas Workers Union objected to the profit sharing scheme because it included an anti-strike clause. They threatened action but, because they were unable to strike without breaking the law, had to persuade the workforce to hand in their notices.

Livesey sealed off the works in a state of siege and marched in 'replacement labour' recruited from a wide area and with the help of unsavoury professional strike breakers. The new workers came in by rail through Westcombe Park Station and proceeded down Blackwall Lane inside a police cordon, to the jeers of the watching crowd. Will Thorne was in Manchester and stayed there until it was clear that the company had won the dispute. Once inside the works the 'new' workers were not allowed to leave. Those that did get over the wall found there a hostile reception and fights and scuffles constantly broke out in Blackwall Lane. 'Old' workers held a bonfire party outside The Pilot pub in Riverway where they burnt an effigy of Livesey as the guy. Rumours of poor conditions inside the works, and, in particular, lice, began to spread. The great gasholder was watched constantly. If gas pressure fell then the company would have lost because contracts with local authorities - largely sympathetic to the strikers - would be broken. It did not fall and, in effect, Livesey had won. He kept the 'new' work force - since legally the action had not been a strike there was no need to take anyone back. Great hardship ensued amongst those who now had lost their jobs.

COPARTNERSHIP

Once the dispute was over Livesey began to expand. Any worker with ideas about trade unions was best advised to keep them to himself. The profit sharing scheme began to evolve into something that Livesey called 'co-partnership' and a whole structure of participation and involvement began to be built up. Workers could take any grievances to 'Co-partnership Committees' which could also recommend changes in a wide range of working practices, and involved themselves in decisions on the various funds - pensions, sickness and so on - managed by company representatives. Co-partnership committees were elected by the workers with an equal representation from management.

In the 1890s Livesey managed to get the company structure altered by a reluctant Board and House of Commons to allow three board members to be directly elected by the co-partners in the workforce. Livesey was nothing if not thorough. On most occasions he was prepared to follow through the logic of what he had done so long as it did not

A Christmas Card sent to all co-partners in South Metropolitan Gas Co. in 1904.

involve giving away any real power. In the years that followed he lectured and wrote constantly about his system. Immediately after the strike his only sympathisers were 'The Liberty and Property Defence League' - the liberty and property in question being their own - and the 'Anti-Picketing League'. The other London gas companies found it more useful to keep in with Will Thorne.

Livesey gradually moved towards a group of idealists on the fringes of the Co-operative movement - the Labour Co-partnership Association.

In 1906 he was to be National President of the Band of Hope and continued to speak on platforms throughout the country on their behalf and for related causes which continued to provide audiences plus bands, flowers and acclaim. The knighthood - and his place in innumerable worthy causes and on Commissions after 1900 - may well have been as much to do with his temperance works as anything. For them there had never been anything to forgive.

South Metropolitan Gas Company.

CO-PARTNERSHIP.

CERTIFICATE OF SERVICE.

This is to Certify that _____ (Pay No. _____

has been in the regular service of the Company at _____

Works from _____ 191__ , to _____ 191__

and is recommended for _____ month's Co-partnership Bonus.

Date _____ 191__ .

Engineer.

EAST GREENWICH WORKS

How did all this effect East Greenwich? Alongside the main gate of the gas works stood the Livesey Institute - a meeting room, hall and theatre. Alongside it was the bowling green, and, in due course a War Memorial. To the south were the allotments and sports facilities.

Most of all, of course, there was the showpiece gas works – almost the biggest in the world, with every department aiming at nothing less than perfection. Dedicated public service to standards that were not only high but encompassed progress and modernity. If that standard was not always reached it was not for lack of saying so. By the time nationalisation came in the late 1940s the South Metropolitan workforce was proud and exclusive. To be a gas worker in Greenwich was to be something very special – better than any other gas workers - better, in fact, than anyone else.

FUEL RESEARCH

George died in 1908 and his place as Company Chairman was taken by Charles Carpenter, an enthusiast for chemical weapons - a trade soon added to the East Greenwich repertoire. The Fuel Research Institute was Government owned and stood adjacent to the South Metropolitan Gas works. Much of its activity is still shrouded in mystery but its role was to do with the investigation of coal based chemicals and the use of coal as a fuel. A Second World War innovation of which they were proud was a smoke screen device.

Local paper advertisement for a South Metropolitan Gas Co. chemical by-product. Dating from the 1940s it features 'Saint George' rather than 'Sir George'!

194

In March 1952 the Duke of Edinburgh, described as 'a good looking young man who drove his large Austin Saloon'[52] visited the station. They explained to him the wartime smoke elimination process as well as experiments on combustion in vortex chambers. He was shown the Calorimeter building for research in domestic heating, which was unique in the world and he met the blacksmith, the longest serving member of staff there. Herbert Morrison visited in 1946 and saw the smoke elimination process and also looked at products which could be obtained from coal and the research into domestic heating from coal.

COLLIERS

At East Greenwich South Metropolitan Gas Co. had their own collier fleet to bring the coal from the Newcastle and Blyth areas. Before the Second World War there were seven vessels- each of 2,000 tons capacity. Four were lost during the war - *Brixton*, which was mined, *Old Charlton*, dive-bombed, *Effra* torpedoed by an E boat and *Catford* mined. The fleet after the war consisted of *Camberwell*, *Redriff*, *Brockley* and *Effra*- A replacement *Effra* was described in 1946 as the last word in luxury as she entered the Thames with her first cargo of coal from Newcastle. She had what then was all the latest equipment -including an echo sounder.

ELECTRICITY

The only trouble with the great gas works was that it was the last one. By the 1880s gas was not new technology – although it put up a very good fight!

The future was with electricity and an electric power station was very soon to stand alongside the gas works.

The East Greenwich tide mill had been almost the latest thing in 1803 - a sophisticated machine to harness the power of the tidal river. It had been overtaken by steam - power generated from coal. The gas works provided another means of power generation from coal. In the early 1890s the old tide mill was replaced by an electrical power station. There was no concept then of the giant power stations which have since grown up and there was no national grid. These early power stations provided electricity to quite small local areas. Many of them were started by the local authorities and many burnt rubbish - for example in Woolwich the local council had built its own power station to make electricity from local waste. In Greenwich a private company undertook this role.

THE FIRST POWER STATION

The new power station built at what became known as Blackwall Point was built by the Blackheath and Greenwich Electric Light Co. It began to supply local people in 1900 by generating power using steam engines fuelled with coal delivered through a big new jetty. The Company's name was changed to the South Metropolitan Electric Light and Power Company Ltd.

They called the new power station 'The Powerhouse'. In 1906 it was extended and when it closed it had a capacity of 15,000 kW. In the 1930s South Metropolitan Electric had showrooms in Lewisham

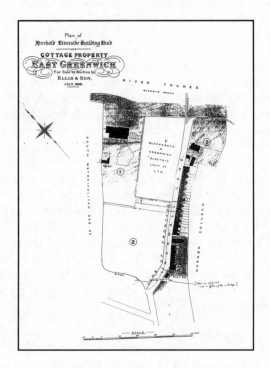

Plan of electricity works built on site
of the East Greenwich tide mill.

Blackheath Standard – almost, but not quite, rivalling the showrooms of South Metropolitan Gas.

In 1901 most of the millponds were still traceable despite having been filled with cinders. A bank '8ft or 10ft high' surrounded the pond so that it could hold water to high tide level. It was thought that the bottom was below ground level.

ANOTHER EXPLOSION

Just before Christmas 1906, there was a sad echo of the 1803 accident when Trevithick's boiler had exploded. William Shaw and James Coombes were working on the power station boilers and were killed as the result of an explosion. Their bodies were blown to pieces, and beyond recognition.

Coombes lived nearby in River Terrace and was a fitter employed at the power station. Mr. Shaw, an inspector from the National Boiler and General Insurance Company, had been called in to examine a leaking drum on the boiler. A leakage of this sort was not unusual and was normally dealt with by caulking. This leak seemed to be very minor, somewhere in the joints rather than the plate of the drum itself. The boiler had been retested regularly. Mr. Shaw was looking for the site of a crack when the explosion occurred.

Both men were killed instantly - James Coombes was identified only by his clothes. The accident was probably caused by an old crack, not visible from the outside of the drum, which had been missed during testing. Later, at the inquest into the deaths members of the jury were clearly very shocked and upset by what they had heard. The original foreman was taken ill after hearing the first evidence and did not return.

The accident was reported in some detail, together with pictures, in the works magazine of the adjacent South Metropolitan Gas Company. It appears that employees of the gas company's other works were invited to Greenwich to see the damage in order that *'those who have charge of boilers. Realise more fully the extent of their responsibility'* - rather than, of course, to see how dangerous electricity was compared to gas! In light of the horrific injuries which were suffered by the two victims this sanctimonious action by the gas company was taking things a bit far!

THE SECOND POWER STATION

The South Metropolitan Electricity Company had decided to replace the power station with a new one before 1939 and it was thus closed and demolished in 1947. Nationalisation overtook them before it was finished and the new Blackwall Point power station opened in 1952.

The power station will be remembered by many local people and it is therefore remarkable that it has proved impossible to trace any archive of this publicly owned site. The whereabouts of records known to have been held before electricity privatisation has become a great mystery.

The new power station was bigger, although limited by its narrow site. For this reason the administration and amenity block was built on the south side of Riverway - connected by an overhead bridge. Equipment used for river navigation was put on the roof of this block by the river authorities and ensured that it was not demolished but remained in a state of dramatic dereliction for many years.

A jetty was built for ships up to 3,000 tons and with facilities so that waste ash and dust could be loaded into barges. Three mills ground the coal into dust before it was fed to each boiler. Three turbo-generators worked to provide the power. In 1953 it was rated the eleventh most efficient power station in the country.

Six months after it closed in June 1980 a group from the Greater London Industrial Archaeology Society visited the site. They were able to actually enter one of the boilers and spend time in the coal handling plant. From the roof they noted 'a magnificent view of the surrounding industrial landscape' – who would have believed that soon all this would have gone and that the site on which they stood would remain derelict for the next twenty years.

19. END OF THE CENTURY

The nineteenth century had been a time of great change on the Greenwich Peninsula. Great efforts had gone into industrialisation but, by the 1890s, things were changing again. Many of the new companies which moved onto sites as the second or third occupants had been established elsewhere and were looking to expand, another trend was the gradual move towards wharfage and haulage activities.

APPLEBY ENGINEERS

This trend can be seen at work in the late 1870s when Appleby Bros. Engineers moved into the area. Appleby were perhaps the largest general engineering company to come to East Greenwich. They were already a successful company and presumably wanted a larger site in the London area. They leased a site

Fig 17.   (For description, &c., see pages 20 to 25.)

*Illustrations from Appleby's 'Handbook of Machinery'
for Greenwich - esentially a catalogue of items they
were prepared to make if ordered.. Above, 'Edith' tank
locomotive and, below, vertical yacht engine. It is very
unlikely that Edith was actually made in Greenwich.*

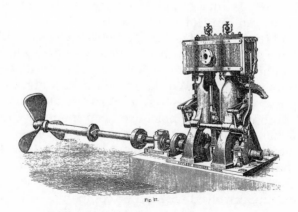

Fig. 27.

from Morden College in 1879 and also took over some of the Victoria Wharf site, still in Bessemer's ownership, and stayed there until 1910. They were to call it Star Wharf.

Appleby had been set up in 1782 at the Renishaw Iron works in Derbyshire. One of the founder's sons, Charles, born in 1828, had been trained at Renishaw. He worked for a Manchester engineering company and then went to Russia to get experience of railways. On his return to England he opened his own engineering works at Emerson Street in Southwark, along with his brother Thomas. It was this factory which, in 1886, moved to Greenwich.

Appleby's catalogue shows an amazing range of goods, which they claimed to manufacture at Greenwich and their other factories. They made railway locomotives and supplied the 2'8" gauge 'Edith' to Robert Campbell of Farringdon in 1871 and they also made their own steam engines. Some were marine engines - in the 1880s they supplied engines to two single screw ships built in Holland for Watkins Tugs, the Australia and the Zealandia. Two Appleby engines are known to have survived into the 1990s:- a single cylinder horizontal steam engine which survived until recently at Sarson's Vinegar Works in Southwark and another is preserved in a Museum at Forncett St. Mary, Norfolk – although it may not have been made in Greenwich. It has been suggested that cranes and hoists were in fact Appleby's most important product. It was cranes that they showed at both the Paris Exhibition of 1876, and the Vienna Exhibition of 1873. They began to become involved with other companies with an interest in cranes and transporters. They acquired the Temperly Transporter Co, in 1908 and a Temperly

Transporter was provided to the adjacent Ordnance Wharf Works of the South Metropolitan Gas Co. around this time.

Appleby came under the control of the Crayford based arms company of Vickers, Son and Maxim, usually known for armaments. Sir Hiram Maxim himself was still alive and lived a few miles away at Bexley. His main work by then was aircraft design and one of his interests was in flying from a fixed point - a 'ride' designed by him still survives in Blackpool. Perhaps a company with expertise in cranes and transporters would have been very useful in this context. Vickers had set up the Glasgow Electric Crane and Hoist Co. together with the Scottish shipping company, Beardmore, and Appleby were also involved with them. The focus of their work began to move away from Greenwich and they concentrated themselves at their works in Leicester. By 1910 they were in financial difficulties and the Greenwich works was at last closed. Their business passed to another Crane Company, Arrol.

LINSEED

At some point in the nineteenth century a seed crushing mill was set up adjacent to Appleby's works. It is this mill, shown on some maps, which has caused a number of historians to claim that there was a windmill on the Peninsula. It was not a windmill but a steam mill and the seed being crushed was almost certainly linseed intended to be used as a source of oil.

The works was also known as the 'London Seed Crushing Co.'. It was to be joined by a major user of linseed oil. Later the works and the wharf became known as 'Greigs' and the name remained. It can only be a matter of speculation if it had any connection with the later Scottish owners of the linoleum works.

LINOLEUM

Linoleum was the universal floor covering of the Victorians, enjoying a rather down-market image today. Oil based floor coverings had evolved during the course of the Century and many linoleum factories had replaced floorcloth factories – in this respect the Greenwich kampultican factory is famous. Linoleum manufacture was, however, the brain child of one man, Frederick Walton who came from near Manchester.

Walton was the son of an inventor and an inventor he also grew up to be. One of his discoveries was oxidised oil – the skin on top of paint. The material he developed could be rolled out onto a suitable backing – using linseed oil and cork and linoleum was the end product. Walton's first factory was in Chiswick in 1861, and he later moved to a bigger works at Staines. The Staines factory is famous with an exhibit in a local museum and a local biographer of Walton. Soon Walton's process was universally used.

The Staines works became independent of Walton and eventually he was to go off and leave it. He seems to

Greenwich

Cover of Greenwich Linoleum Pattern Book.
With kind permission Forbo Nairn. PLC

have quarrelled with his managers over new developments and determined to go somewhere else with his
new invention. That somewhere else was to be Greenwich.

A lease was taken out on Victoria Wharf from the
owners. By 1910 the works had become immense and
was eventually to be on two sites - the other slightly
further north. It made about 20 miles of linoleum
each week – a year's output would have stretched to
Warsaw! They used a mixture of cork, oils and
colouring. Each sheet was made of tens of thousands

of tiny pieces – made up in an original pattern into a template by specialist craftsmen. A vast machine – 50 feet high and weighing 400 tons – produced huge sheets of lino in six different colours. These sheets were then cut and welded into the different designs.

The works operated from two sites – part of Bethell's Wharf was also used, although the date of the expansion is not clear. The company was taken over by Michael Nairn Co. of Kirkaldy in the 1920s and seems to have been closed in 1934 or shortly afterwards.

A General View of the Redpath Brown, structural steel works taken from the from the river in the early year of the works. With thanks to Arthur Turner

20.A NEW CENTURY

Just before the start of the twentieth century the Blackwall Tunnel had opened on the Greenwich Peninsula. Built for horse and pedestrian transport, it transformed the area, making road access throughout the area easier. It connected north and south banks of the river in a dramatic way – a cultural shock to many South Londoners!

A start was also being made in the great changes which would come during the century and in particular in the way in which industry was powered. The small local power station was aimed at domestic lighting – but it was an omen for the future. Another sign of the revolution to come was the opening of the first garage for motor transport – nearby a slaughter house for horses.

The Blackwall Tunnel itself has been well described elsewhere – there is no need to add it here. It could be said that the new industry of the Greenwich

Peninsula has become traffic! The tunnel and its construction mark a point of change in the area – and a long period of gradual decline.

Before the first world war some large companies moved to the Greenwich Peninsula – Molassine, Redpath Brown and Delta - to set a pattern for the next fifty years. The years of change were over and the Peninsula was settling down. If the following chapters are a rather boring list of sites it is because things had become rather boring – big companies, no doubt doing a good job but no excitement.

REDPATH BROWN – STRUCTURAL STEEL

Redpath Brown was an Edinburgh based company dealing with structural steel. In 1903 they decided to open a London branch and moved to a hitherto unused site to the south of Riverway. Spoil from the Blackwall Tunnel had been dumped there and considerable work was needed to make the ground acceptable for a large works.

In 1929 the Company merged with Dorman Long and later a site known as 'Dorman Long' was added to the Greenwich works. This seems to have operated only as a depot and to have been a completely separate establishment.

Redpath Brown provided the structural steel for many important buildings in London from the Greenwich works. This almost certainly included the Festival Hall, several power stations and other major buildings. A local example is the railway bridge built as an emergency after the St.John's railway disaster of 1956. They also undertook an important role in the second World War in the construction of landing craft.The works was nation-alised with the rest of the steel industry and was

DELTA METAL - BRONZE

The largest and best known metal producer on the Peninsula was the Delta Metal Company. Delta were, and are, a very important company which was still in business at their Greenwich site well into the 1980s, specialising in a range of bronzes.

 Alexander Dick had come to England from Europe in the 1880s. He was of British descent, but born and educated in Germany and had worked in Spain and France. In England he established the Phosphor Bronze Company in New Cross and managed it until 1882. He formed similar companies in other European coun-tries at around the same time. In 1883 he began to work on brass and other alloys and, in particular, added iron to brass. The resulting alloy was named 'Delta Metal' and this name was the registered trade-mark for other alloys made by the company. Dick also adapted an extrusion process for the production of brass rod. This process was first used at New Cross in the early 1890s and in 1905 the Greenwich site was opened as the Extruded Metals Company Ltd. During the next seventy years the works grew

to take over much of the area along the north eastern riverfront as other works closed down.

The First World War brought Delta increased business and also competition. The Dick family continued to manage the company throughout consolidation up to 1940. In the Second World War metal manufactured at East Greenwich found its way into other works up and down the country. Delta boasted that '*by the end of the war there was hardly even a repair garage of any size in the land which did not have lathes, drilling and milling machines installed and working day and night turning out metal parts for war uses...the parts were produced from Delta extruded bars*'. Their products were used in '*fuses and primers for shells, for parts and fittings of guns and torpedoes, for searchlights, and Radar apparatus, and all the other innumerable scientific instruments, telephone parts, aircraft fittings, ship construction angles, tee and channel bars, and other sections for ships' fittings.. used in craft of all kinds from the largest battleships to the smallest launches; components of vehicles from tanks to lorries, of speedometers, lighting equipment and "Mulberry," "Pluto" and "Fido"*.

They boasted a 500 ft long jetty with 16 feet depth of water at high water. The dangers of river wharfage work had been demonstrated in 1935 when a 25 ton crane toppled into the river while undergoing special tests for an insurance company to see if it was safe. The crane driver was killed – his body could not be recovered until the 150 ton floating crane owned by the Port of London Authority had arrived. After the war, however, Delta were to use much of their huge site for warehousing but the company itself moved on from strength to strength, to become a successful multi-national. Experimental work on bronzes continued at Greenwich throughout the 1960s and 1970s but this works, where their large-scale manufacture started, was closed apparently unnoticed in the 1980s. Some work was undertaken in Greenwich on the old Johnson and Phillips site in Charlton, but in the 1990s Delta has left Greenwich altogether.

TILBURY DREDGING AND CONTRACTING

Tilbury Dredging and Contracting are a large and important Thames company with several depots up and down the river. In 1906 they opened a depot in Banning Street next to Pipers. Several other such companies were to find sites on the Greenwich Peninsula over the next sixty years and were essentially a service industry taking over from the manufacturing companies which had previously occupied these sites. When manufacturing industry and the port finally collapsed, they moved out – leaving behind them the dereliction which has continued ever since. There were many other such companies in this period – for example, Thames Export Packing is another.

MOLASSINE

In the twentieth century the Greenwich waterfront became known as a place of very bad smells. In a history of the Molassine works written in the 1950s the company said how everyone who went past on the river knew them from the dramatic sight of their large molasses tanks – local people were more likely to know them by the dramatic smells which came from the works!

Molassine produced animal foods based on molasses. They operated from the red stone office block near the entrance to the Blackwall tunnel – a building of which they very proud. They were best known for the pet food 'Vims – *All dogs love them*' but they also made cattle and poultry food each with its own catchy trade name.

SHAW LOVELL

Lovell's, from Bristol, were yet another service industry. Lovell's Wharf is very noticeable to anyone walking eastwards along the riverside from Ballast Quay. The company had been ships' agents since 1869 and had developed a special relationship with some Bristol shipowners. They had been in Greenwich since before 1922 and after that date they began to consolidate here, eventually taking over the lease on their site and moving onto neighbouring wharves. They moved their head office to Greenwich after the Second World War and in the 1960s built the office block, which still stands there. In 1975 they brought a Butters Crane to Greenwich from the Dublin Custom House. Most of their business concerned the transfer of various metals from ship to lorry. The site had became too small for them by the 1970s and they were eventually forced to close.

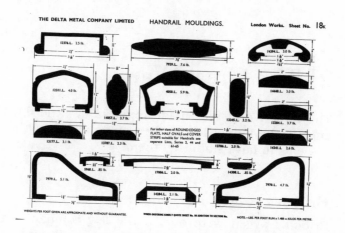

Detail from a Delta Catalogue. Kind permission Delta Metal plc.

21. The Great War

The First World War made remarkably little differ-
ence to the industries on the Peninsula. If anything
it seems to have stabilised them.

British Oxygen

British Oxygen were one of the few companies to
move to Greenwich during the war.   It was yet
another established company siting   a depot in
Greenwich.

The works was on a site to the North of Tunnel
Avenue, redeveloped for housing in 1998. It probably covered some of the site previously used by the
ammunition works.

British Oxygen was set up by the Brin brothers in
1887 in Westminster and Glasgow and went on to
become a successful multi-national.   There is some
unexplained connection with Frederick Walton of the
Inlaid Linoleum Company. (see above). Historians
who have attempted to evaluate Walton's life have
found several mysterious episodes.   One of these

was his claim to have worked for British Oxygen. He could not have done so in Greenwich but the fact of his large linoleum factory being so near to the British Oxygen site raises a number of questions.

MORE WHARFAGING

During the first world war period the trend towards riverside sites being taken up by wharfingers and river service industries continued. British and Foreign Wharf Ltd. took over Greig's Wharf – where the linseed crushing mill had been. United Ship Builders and Repairers Ltd moved onto Providence Wharf.

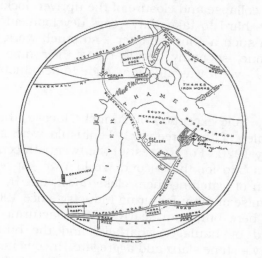

22. THE REST OF THE TWENTIETH CENTURY

The twentieth century continued to be worthy and boring with a gradual decline as industries closed – to be replaced by depots and service industries. It was a long slow way down which ended with the sudden collapse and closure of the upriver docks. If it seems hard to take sixty years development and work in such a short chapter – so much work was been done, so many people using their time and energies – yet it was all a long slide to deindustrialisation.

With the sole exception of Tunnel Glucose, the big companies of the Greenwich Peninsula were all in place by 1920. For the rest of the twentieth century – with a blip for the Second World War – it was a question of watching them close down, one by one. The demise of manufacturing industry since 1900 is shown here only too clearly. Manufacturing was replaced by haulage, wharfage, and the building industry – stone slabs and aggregate. Incomers were mostly small and mostly short lived. The vitality so clear of the 1860s had been replaced – with what?

DEAD HORSES

When the area was semi-rural there were many horses grazing in the fields who earned their living in the cab trade. As time went by many of the horses to be seen in the fields were actually waiting their turns at the knackers, Harrison Barber, in Blackwall Lane. Most of the information about this slaughterhouse comes from the report of a suicide – an employee who used the patent killer on himself.

What replaced the horses was the internal combustion engine. Garages and motor repair depots were opening quickly. In 1933 the opening of Crossways Service Station was a sign of the times. This was next to the knackers – so the horses' last moments on earth would be the sight of their real killer - the motor car.

OTHER INDUSTRIES

It would be dishonest not to mention some of the industries which did move on to the Peninsula in the sixty years after the first world war. There was, for instance, A.& S. Henry & Co., sack manufacturers and Stewart Carbonising on Morden Wharf .

SWEET SUCCESS

There is one success story among the industries which came to Greenwich in the 1930s. This is the flourishing sugar refinery, known in the 1990s as Amylum UK but previously Tunnel Glucose. Sugar is very much an industry of London's riverside.

Most of the big names in sugar refining have been here - Tate and Lyle are still in operation on the other side of the river. Tunnel Refineries were specialists, making glucose syrups to specialist formulae to sell to trade outlets. In this they have been very successful with a big modern plant which does credit to the area – why complain too much about the smell!

They opened in 1934. In 1998 the refinery covered 27 acres and included a related distillery. They are very proud of their record in enhancing the environment of the riverside.

Perhaps we should take a quick glance at the other big factory still in operation. At Enderby's wharf Alcatel are now in possession of the factory which has been producing telecommunications equipment since the birth of the industry.

MORE SERVICE INDUSTRY

These final few paragraphs chart some of the industries which moved onto the wharves as manufacturing industry moved away. For instance in 1927 Eastwoods, the wharfage company, were situated on Greig's Wharf. They are a famous river haulage company – through the early nineteenth century managed by the redoubtable Jane Eastwood. They had a brickworks at Shoeburyness and had a fleet of fifty sailing barges.

Depots for everything flourished. In 1951 the National Benzole Co. moved onto the site where Bethell had had his chemical works. On Victoria Wharf the linoleum factory was replaced by the Metropolitan Storage and Trade Co. Ltd and in 1970 by the Victoria Deep Water Terminal. This was a specialist wharf for handling containers. In 1987 40,000 boxes were being handled on the wharf every year – well below its actual capacity. The two gantry cranes, painted in brilliant colours, were a landmark on the river and hated by incoming yuppies on the Isle of Dogs.

Morden Wharf became a warehousing complex in the 1950s owned by Taylor Brothers Wharfage. They boasted a quay for ships up to 270 feet in length with three waterside cranes and ten overhead cranes. Even Delta gave over part of their enormous site to warehousing. The list of these companies is enormous. Each advertised with pride their vast floor areas, the length of their wharf, and its handling capacity.

AND AGGREGATES

In the 1980s many of the wharves went over to aggregates. When Delta closed in the 1970s the site was taken by Civil and Marine - which specialised in sea dredged aggregates. At that time they operated two 5,000-ton sand and gravel dredgers from a headquarters in Purfleet. In 1995 they were bought by the Hanson Group and at that time had a bulk carrier and four dredgers.

THE MITRE

A cheerful interlude was provided by events at the Mitre Pub - built in the 1880s on Blackwall Lane to provide something for thirsty gas workers. As the population of drinkers dwindled in the 1960s it became a venue for local bands - in particular the very wonderful Wally Butcher and the Laughing Gravy Orchestra.

International jazz star Dudu Pukwana played to a miniscule audience on Sunday lunch times.

Eventually it became home to Malcolm Hardee's notorious Tunnel Club (Alternative Comedians v. The Eltham Boys). Once all the acts had been booed off, Malcolm would usually do anything on stage that the audience asked.

South Met's. Festival of Britain logo

23.GREENWICH MARSH IN THE YEAR 2000

Nothing exists in a void, even the future. If we accept that time exists then we have to see how each thing develops after the next or it makes no sense to us.

This book has been an attempt to show how the Greenwich Peninsula developed and to suggest here that the Dome is almost the logical next step. It is after all an industry providing entertainment and information for those who want to buy it. It is different to the other industries only in so far as people have to call and get what they are buying on site – previously things were delivered!

The past remains with us, whatever we do. The popular view in the late 1990s has insisted that pollution is, almost the only, the legacy of past industry. Sorry, but pollution really isn't the point. The actual legacy is complex and much more rele-vant to the present than that. Going on about pollution - and nothing else - is in fact an insult to those who worked hard to leave us the whole world that we live in now.

Greenwich is full of sites which pull the tourists in. Its working areas have been disregarded as mundane. Even Iain Sinclair has ignored the marsh.

Nothing is old and romantic, but we live among the accretions of the past and we owe it some respect.

The East Greenwich Gas holder seen across the townscape of East Greenwich. Drawing by kind permission Spatial Logic.

NOTES

1.Michael Baldwin, The River and the Downs. Kent's Unsung Corner.
2.Letter from Rennie. (LMA)
3. David Kynaston. The City of London. A World of its Own. 1815-1890.
4.Ordnance Dept. Records (PRO)
5.O.Hogg. The Royal Arsenal.
6. Kentish Mercury
7.S.Parkes, A Treatise on Chemistry.
8. Muriel Searle. The Importance of Being Bugsby. Port of London. Jan 1974.
9. Rod Helps. Piracy on the Thames. Bygone Kent. 16/4.
10.Greenwich Commission of Sewers (LMA)
11.Wendy Hinde. George Canning.
12. Philosophical Magazine. Vol.16.
13.Francis Trevithick, Life of Richard Trevithick.
14.As above.
15.As above.
16. Philosophical Magazine. Vol.
17. Greenwich Commission of Sewers (LMA)
18.A. & N. Clow. The Chemical Revolution.
19.Sally Jenkinson. Enderby Wharf.
20.J.L.Kieve, Electric Telegraph
21.As above.
22.Kentish Mercury
23.As above.
24.Morden College Trustee's Minutes
25.Post Office Directory
26.Mechanics' magazine 7/1840.
27.As above
28.As above
29.Trade Names, courtesy Unilever.
30.Neil Rhind. Blackheath Village and Environs.
31.Kentish Mercury
32.Henry Bessemer, An Autobiography.
33.As above.
34.Frederick Walton. Infancy and Development of Linoleum Floorcloth.
35.Adrian Caruana. Alexander Theophilus Blakeley. Ord. Soc.Jrnl.
36.Warren Ripley. Artillery and Ammunition of the Civil War.
37.As above
38.Kentish Mercury & Report of Inspector of Explosives.
39.Kentish Mercury
40 It is understood a book on Emery is under preparation by Prof. Jeremy Mouat, Athabasca University.
41.Philip Banbury, Shipbuilders of the Thames and Medway
42.P. Barry. Dockyard Economy and Naval Power
43.As above.
44.Kentish Mercury
45.David MacGregor, The Tea Clippers
46.House of Lords Enquiry into South Met. Gas Co. 1881
47.Bob Roberts. Coasting Bargemaster
48.Dolphin Sailing Barge Museum.
49.Pat O'Driscoll in private correspondence
50.Angerstein Wharf. Southern Railway Magazine Dec 1925 & Nov. 1951.
51.Journal of Gas Lighting/Co-partnership Journal.

BIBLIOGRAPHY

Footnotes have not been included in the text except for direct quotations. The following books and archives have been the main sources of material, books used for reference only are not included. In addition a major source has been the local press - mainly the Kentish Mercury - and the very large collection of cuttings, pamphlets and ephemera held in the Woodlands Local History Library, London Borough of Greenwich.

Angerstein Wharf, Southern Railway Magazine, December 1925 & November 1951.

Edward Ballard, Report of the Effluvium Nuisance arising in connection with various manufacturing & other industry, HMSO, London, 1882.

Edward Ballard, Report on the alleged nuisance from noxious trades carried on the shores of the River Thames from Blackwall Reach to Erith Reach, Local Government Board, nd.

P.Barry, Dockyard Economy and Naval Power, 1864.

W.V.Bartlett, 'The River & the Marsh at East Greenwich', TGLA, Vol.7, No.2, 1964-5, pp.68-84.

Sir Henry, Bessemer, FRS, An Autobiography. With a concluding chapter, London Offices of 'Engineering', 1905.

Adrian Caruana, Alexander Theophilus Blakeley, Ordnance Society Journal, Vol. 4, 1992.

J.L.Filmer, The Bromley Palace and Coles Child. Lord of the Manor of Bromley. 1846-1873, Bromley Local History, No. 5, 1980, pps 21-40.

Olinthus Gregory, Mechanics, London,1806.

Sally Jenkinson, Enderby Wharf., nd.

Patrick Joyce, Patronage and Poverty in Merchant Society. The History of Morden College, Blackheath. 1695 to the present. Gresham Books. 1982.

Michael Kerney, The development of an Early Victorian

Artisan Estate in east Greenwich. Trans Greenwich and Lewisham, Antiq. Soc., 1983/4, Vol.IX No. 6, pps. 299-313.

Barbara Ludlow, Social Conditions on Greenwich Marsh 1837-1901, TGLAS, Vii/3, 1968, pp 130-141.

Georg Lunge. Coal Tar and Ammonia, 1881.

Barbara Ludlow 'The Early History of Coombe Farm', nd

David Mcgregor, The Tea Clippers

John Merrett, Three Miles Deep, Hamish Hamilton, 1958.

R.G.Purnell,. The Delta Story, nd, Delta Metal Co.

Neil Rhind, Blackheath Village and & Environs 1790-1970. Vols. 1 & 2. Blackheath, 1983.

Muriel Searle, The Importance of Being Bugsby. Port of London, Jan 1974.

Telcon Story, Telcon. n.d.

Francis Trevithick, Life of Richard Trevithick, Spon, 1872.

Universal Directory, 1791

Frederick Walton, Infancy and Development of Linoleum Floorcloth, 1925, MS.

Jenny West, Gunpowder, Government, & War in the Mid-Eighteenth Century, RHS Studies in History 63, 1991,

ARCHIVE SOURCES
City of London Record Office
Greater London Record Office
Guildhall Library
Kent County Record Office
Kirkaldy Museum and Art Gallery
London Borough of Greenwich Local History Library
London Borough of Southwark Local History Library
Martin Collection
Morden College
Public Record Office
Tyne and Wear Archive
Worshipful Company of Drapers
Worshipful Company of Mercers

MS
Tim Smith. Text on Appleby Bros.
John Day. Notes on A.T.Blakely
Maj Wagstaffe, Davies papers

BY THE SAME AUTHOR
Mary Mills, The Early Gas Industry and its Residual Products in East London, PhD Thesis, Open University, 1995.
Mary Mills, Profit Sharing in the South Metropolitan Gas Company, M.Phil Thesis, Thames Polytechnic, 1995.
Mary Mills, The Hills Family, Bygone Kent, 18/3, March 1997, pp 169-172.
Mary Mills, Steam Cars made in Greenwich and Run In Kent, Bygone Kent, 18/8 Sept, 1997, pp.511-516.
Mary Mills, John Beale and Joshua Beale, Inventors from Greenwich Marsh, Bygone Kent, 18/6, June 1997, pp 329-333
Mary Mills, The Millennium Site - Who built the Gas Works, Bygone Kent, 17/5, May 1996, pp. 287-290.
Mary Mills, The Millennium Site - Bad Smells on Greenwich Marsh, Bygone Kent, 17/7 July 1996, pp. 432-437.
Mary Mills, An Industrial Site in East Greenwich, Bygone Kent, 17/12 Dec, 1996, pp. 735-740.
Mary Mills, The Millennium Site, Part Three, New East Greenwich, Bygone Kent, 17/8 August 1996, pp. 461-464.
Mary Mills, The Gas Workers Strike in South London, South London Record, No.4, 1989.
Mary Mills, Heavy Chemicals on Deptford Creek, Jrnl. Greenwich Historical Society, Vol. 1, No.6, 1997, pp. 173-180.
Mary Mills, An Industrial Accident at East Greenwich, Bygone Kent, 17/11, Nov. 1996, pp. 661-664.
Mary Mills', The Explosive Magazine at Greenwich, Bygone Kent, Vol. 18. No.12
Mary Mills, The Greenwich Gunpowder Depot, Gunpowder Mills Study Group, No. 21.
Mary Mills, A Mystery Steel Works, Bygone Kent. V..20. No.1. pp.37-43

Mary Mills, Nathan Thompson and the Wooden Nutmeg. Bygone Kent. V..19. No.5. pp.277-181

Mary Mills, Gunpowder. Inspection and Death, Bygone Kent. V..19. No.1. pp.25-29

Mary Mills, A Breach in the Sea Wall, Bygone Kent. V.19. No.4. pp 233-237

Mary Mills, Drugs, Guns and High Finance. Bygone Kent. V.19.No.7 391-397.

Mary Mills, Greenwich Marsh Flood Defences. Newcomen Bulletin, No. 170, April 1998.

Mary Mills, Greenwich Inland Linoleum, Bygone Kent, V.20.No.3. pp 177-182

Mary Mills, The Dock That Never Was, Bygone Kent, V.20, No.4. pp. 213-219

THANKS

Thanks are owed to a great many people, most of whom are listed below. Anyone who has been omitted should accept my apologies. Mary Mills

Bob Aspinall
Richard Buchanon
Beverley Burford
Pam Carr
Bob Carr
Adrian Caruana
Howard Chard
Alan Crocker
Glynis Crocker
John Day
Delta Metal (Sec's Dept.)
Nicholas Dent
Richard Ellham
Bill Firth
Chris Grabham
Peter Guillery
Michael Hills
Patrick Hills
Richard Hills
Brian Hilsdon
Brian Hope
Jim Hughes
Marcus Humphrey
Sally Jenkinson
Stephen Johnson
Michael Kearney
Peter Kent
Fred Lindop
Barbara Ludlow
Derek Matthews

Alan Mills
Terry Mitchell
Kay Murch
Patricia O'Driscoll
Ralph Parsons
Hugh Perks
David Perrett
Denis Postle
Graham Reeve
Len Riley
Neil Rhind
Gerrylyn Roberts
Wendy Schnur
Bob Score
Tim Smith
Roger Strugnell
Brian Sturt
Pat Sturt
Malcolm Tucker
Andrew Turner
Arthur Turner
Ian Turner
Maj Wagstaff
Tom Wareham
Julian Watson
John West
Malcolm Whiteside
Elizabeth Wiggins
Elizabeth Wood
David Wood

I would in particular like to pay tribute to the late Adrian Caruana and Jim Hughes, for their support and help.

INDEX

THE AUTHOR

Mary Mills has lived in Greenwich for 30 years - in a house over-looking Greenwich Marsh. A life long interest in the area and its industry led her to undertake an M.Phil at what was then Thames Polytechnic, about George Livesey and the East Greenwich Gas works, and later, a PhD about local industry. She is an Executive Member of the Greater London Industrial Archaeology Society and Secretary of the Greenwich Industrial History Society. In between that she has, until recently, worked for Docklands Forum – a community organisation which monitors regeneration in East London.

THE ARTIST

Peter Kent, whose designs are on the front and back cover,
works from his riverside studio in Greenwich which has com-
manding views of the western side of the Greenwich Peninsula
– and has witnessed the construction of the Dome. Over the last
thirty years Peter has illustrated and written about the enormous
changes along the Thames and Docklands. His interest in this
intriguing area stems from obtaining a PLA pass to the Docks
while he was a student at the Regent Street School of Art some
forty years ago.

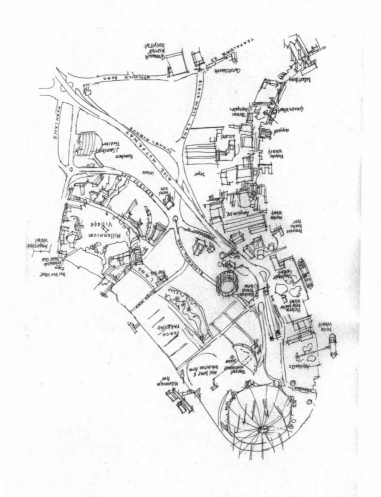